HUMILITY PRACTICE

*27 Ways to Think Less of Yourself—
and of Yourself Less*

Jacob Hudgins

Humility Practice: 27 Ways to Think Less of Yourself—and of Yourself Less

Cover designed by Bre Vaughn
Cover photo by Paula Schmidt

Visit my website at www.jacobhudgins.com

Printed in the United States of America

ISBN-13 978-1-7352970-0-2

CONTENTS

INTRODUCTION

"Thus says the LORD:
'Heaven is my throne,
And the earth is my footstool;
What is the house that you would build for me, and what is the place of
  my rest?
All these things my hand has made,
And so all these things came to be, declares the LORD.
But this is the one to whom I will look:
He who is humble and contrite in spirit
And trembles at my word'"(Isa 66:1-2).

I SAIAH'S STATEMENT IS A JAW-DROPPER. God—to whom outer space is merely a throne room—speaks. The earth—which none of us will likely ever leave during our lifetimes—is simply the stool for his feet. He is a God too big to be contained in any house man could fashion, no matter how grand.

What is the focus of a God like *that*? What interests *him*? *"But this is the one to whom I will look: he who is humble and contrite in spirit and trembles at my word."* Almighty God pays the closest attention to the humble and lowly person. God loves the humble.

A Bible Theme that Resonates

The Bible's teaching on pride is one of its least controversial. "*A haughty look*" is number one on Solomon's list of seven things the LORD hates (Prov 6:16–17). "*Pride goes before destruction, and a haughty spirit before a fall*"(Prov 16:18). The only frustration with this proverb is that there are some occasions when we wish it would come true sooner. The Bible shows us people who grow proud and suffer for it (Nabal, Haman, Korah). We feel little sadness at watching their stories play out.

In the New Testament, Jesus frequently condemns pride with one of his favorite sayings: "*Everyone who exalts himself will be humbled, but the one who humbles himself will be exalted*"(Luke 18:14, Matt 23:12, Luke 14:11). Implicit in his statement is the idea that *this is more than just the natural consequence of pride. God is the one who does the exalting and humbling.*

Later in the New Testament, James and Peter both quote from a statement in Proverbs: "*God opposes the proud, but gives grace to the humble*"(1 Pet 5:5, James 4:6). God makes the proud his enemies. His favor is for those who are willing to lower themselves before him.

This is a Bible theme that resonates. We *want* this to be true. Arrogance is universally distasteful and annoying. Even as modern American culture tends to reward the brash and cocky, we still know that this is a difficult trait to live with. Proud people think they always know best. They cannot work in teams. They do not relate well to others because others must either respect them or rival them. They do not grow. They cannot take advice. They do not respect others' ideas. They are hard to talk to.

So when God tells us that pride is evil, tends to destruction, and will be destroyed by God, we cheer! But that joy rests on the assumption that *we* are never the proud ones! John Seldon laments, "Humility is a virtue all men preach, none practice, and yet everybody is content to hear. The master thinks it good doctrine for his servants, the laity for the clergy, and the clergy for the laity"[1]. We want this to be true—but only for others.

It is obvious that our broader culture is not helping us learn humility. In his book *The Road to Character*, David Brooks compiles a set of disturbing surveys:

- In 1950, 12 percent of high school seniors considered themselves a very important person. In 2005, that number had risen to 80 percent.

- On a narcissism test containing statements like "I like to be the center of attention" and "Someone should write a biography about me," the median narcissism score has risen 30 percent in the last two decades.

- In a 1976 survey of people's life goals, fame ranked 15th out of 16. In 2007, 51% of young people listed fame as one of their top personal goals.[2]

Ironically, our culture teaches us to despise the caricatures of pride while pushing us toward them. We revile the greed and self-centeredness of Ebenezer Scrooge—yet we scramble for money and

---

[1] Cited in Worthington, p. 17.
[2] Brooks, p. 6-7.

power, stepping over others in the process. We despise the boss who micromanages his employees and refuses to share power—yet we sincerely believe that if everyone would do things *our* way, it would all go more smoothly. We criticize the athlete who attributes all his success to his own greatness and beats his chest—yet we insist that our own success is a result of our hard work and talent.

Meanwhile, technological advancements have made it easier for us to have every opportunity for pride and fame at our fingertips. The most common use of our ubiquitous cellphone cameras is pictures of ourselves—SELFies. We are the stars. Our desires are deified. Companies market to us. Churches cater to us. Politicians make us promises. Life in such a climate makes everyone feel that someone should write a biography about us. After all, I am a special, important person doing something awesome.

We are caught between a visceral distaste of pride and a culture that encourages it. The trouble with humility is in remembering that *we* need it—and in learning *how* to get and keep it.

What Is This Book?

I have always struggled with the *practical* side of humility. When instructed to be humble, I was never told what to *do*. "Be humble" doesn't help much; the verb here is "be," not "do." Yet I began to notice that my humility would come in waves. There were times when I could tell that I wasn't thinking of myself as much—or when I wasn't as boastful or as competitive with others—and then times when my pride got out of hand. It occurred to me that there were certain behaviors that triggered a deeper sense of humility, usually immediately. Left to my own devices, I became more and more proud until I reached a crisis that revealed my ego. I wanted a way I could regularly refocus on humility.

So I began to collect those actions and experiences that helped me gain flashes of humility. This book puts those things together as a set of humility disciplines.

Most of the practices detailed in the book center around a few stubborn aspects of pride: self-focus, condescension, and ingratitude. I am sure that there are more humility practices that would be helpful. Feel free to add your own to this list.

Each chapter has the same sections. I briefly introduce the idea, then show where Scripture advocates it ("The Biblical Connection"). One of the most interesting aspects of this material is that because most of the practices are so simple, we think they are easy. I have tried to give a sense of the difficulty of actually living the practice with the section "Why Is This Hard?". Each chapter then asks the question "How Does This Help with Humility?", linking the practical and the abstract. At the conclusion of the chapter, I have added my "Field Notes." As I tried to live these principles, I felt that some observations of my experiences might be helpful to you as you put them into practice.

A couple of cautions: These practices are not to be done to "show" anyone—be it ourselves, God, or others—that we are humble. Also, these practices are not activities we perform once, master them, and then check them off the list. In fact, thinking we've become humble is a surefire sign that we haven't.

God exalts the humble. Let's get to work.

A PRIDE PRIMER

WHAT DOES IT MEAN TO BE PROUD? Before we pursue the essence of humility, let's see the lay of the land ahead.

Pride as Self-Focus ("I'm great")

Pride manifests as a preoccupation with ourselves. We spend the majority of our time concentrating on our own goals, hopes, and dreams. We constantly take our own emotional temperature to discover whether we are happy or sad or bored or frustrated. We think so much of ourselves that we assume that there is little to discover outside ourselves. We begin to value our own thoughts and opinions more than those of others. We begin to think we are great.

Paul warns us: "*For by the grace given to me I say to everyone among you not to think of himself more highly than he ought to think, but to think with sober judgment, each according to the measure of faith that God has assigned*"(Rom 12:3). Not only does Paul imply that we tend to think more of ourselves than is justified, but he states plainly that what we are is a gift from God. This is important because self-focus often leads to revisionist history: we got to be as great as we are because we worked so hard! We ignore the sacrifices others made and blessings others gave that contributed to the goodness in our lives. We just assume we deserve it all. After all, we sure are great. Just ask us!

In another place Paul asks a penetrating question: *"What do you have that you did not receive? If then you received it, why do you boast as if you did not receive it?"* (1 Cor 4:7). Scripture teaches us that all that we have is a gift from God. This puts the focus on him rather than us. It eliminates boasting because we are only recipients. But when we begin to think so much of ourselves that we decide we are great, pride thrives.

Pride as Comparison ("I'm better")

Usually we seek validation for our good feelings about ourselves by looking around at others. We might make mistakes, but so do others! We especially seek out those to whom we know we compare favorably. We may not be perfect, but at least we're better than that guy!

This is a truly stunning feat of mental gymnastics. Consider God's description of his people—and how they justify themselves by comparisons—in Isaiah:

> *"I spread out my hands all the day to a rebellious people, who walk in a way that is not good, following their own devices; a people who provoke me to my face continually, sacrificing in gardens and making offerings on bricks; who sit in tombs, and spend the night in secret places; who eat pig's flesh, and broth of tainted meat is in their vessels; who say, 'Keep to yourself, do not come near me,*

for I am too holy for you.' These are a smoke in my
nostrils, a fire that burns all the day"(Isa 65:2-5).

These people are thoroughly wicked. They pursue idolatry. They ignore God's rules about defilement. They eat unclean food. Then they turn around to others and tell them to stay away. "*I am too holy for you.*" As long as they can find someone to look down on, they consider themselves righteous—and far better than others.

These kinds of comparisons distract us from seeing ourselves rightly. As long as we look at others, we don't really look at ourselves. Jesus warns us about focusing on the speck in someone else's eye while ignoring the beam in our own (Matt 7:3). Comparison does not usually leave room for self-examination and improvement, since we are too busy condescending.

Pride as Exemption ("I'm different")

In advanced cases, pride shows up as the belief that the ordinary rules of life don't apply to a person as great as me.

The night of his betrayal, Jesus warns his disciples that "*You will all fall away because of me this night*"(Matt 26:31). The group seems stunned by this—except for Peter. "*Peter answered him, 'Though they all fall away because of you, I will never fall away'*"(Matt 26:33). Peter is perfectly willing to throw the other disciples under the bus. *They* might forsake you, Jesus, but *I* would never do something like that! Peter is convinced that he is different—more committed, more dependable, more passionate. He cannot see a scenario where Jesus' words are true of him. And in his feeling of exemption, Peter sets himself up for a fall.

This sense of exemption—"the rules don't apply to me"—occurs in response to general rules of life too. There is a way the world works. Certain actions bring consequences. But prideful people always want to bypass these natural results in their case. We want to eat whatever we want and never gain weight. We want to neglect other people and still have great relationships. We want to drink and drive and make it home safely. Some bad things might happen to other people, but they'll never happen to us! We're different!

Paul speaks to this as well: "*Do not be deceived: God is not mocked, for whatever one sows, that will he also reap. For the one who sows to his own flesh will from the flesh reap corruption, but the one who sows to the Spirit will from the Spirit reap eternal life*"(Gal 6:7-8). We will reap what we sow. We are not somehow different. That is true in physical and spiritual things. God will not be mocked by making miraculous exceptions just for us.

You Might Be Proud...

C.S. Lewis describes pride as "the great sin". Pride "leads to every other vice: it is the complete anti-God state of mind"[3]. He has the demon Screwtape strategize about a Christian's pride: "Your patient has become humble; have you drawn attention to the fact?"[4] Pride is so insidious that even when we are making efforts to correct it, we can be drawn to it.

---

[3] Lewis, *Mere Christianity*, p. 103.
[4] Lewis, *The Screwtape Letters*, p. 224.

One of the biggest challenges of pride is that proud people never think *they* are the ones with a pride problem. It is vital for us to openly consider whether we might be proud. You might be proud...

- If you think you've earned what you have.
- If you think your way is the only way.
- If you think you know better than God.
- If you think you're in control.
- If you think you don't need to change.
- If you can't say you're sorry.
- If you think other people don't respect you enough.
- If you think you should be in charge.
- If you resent when things are not perfect in your life.
- If you are jealous when someone else gets attention.
- If you are angry when you don't get credit.

How can we do better than this? How can we pursue humility?

CHAPTER 1: CONFESS A SIN

C HRISTIANS KNOW THAT SIN EXISTS—and that it is a bad thing. We even know other people who have sinned. We see stories about their sins in the news and sometimes feel the sting of their evil directed at us. Confessing others' sins is easy.

We might even be willing to admit that *we* have sinned—just in some distant time and place, with details that we don't want to go into. We can talk a lot about sin and how awful it is; we just don't want to talk about our own sin. Instead, we make excuses, blame others, and rationalize our behavior.

Humility comes when we confess our sin.

The Biblical Connection

When we have done wrong, we essentially have two options. We can choose to live in denial about it or we can confess it and ask for God's forgiveness. Proverbs tells us that "*whoever conceals his transgressions will not prosper, but he who confesses and forsakes them will obtain mercy*" (Prov 28:13). "Concealing" our sins means that we follow the well-trod path of trying to get away with it. We might tell out-and-out lies, like Gehazi (*"your servant went nowhere,"* 2 Kings 5:25). We might minimize our role in the sin and portray ourselves as victims, like Aaron (*"I threw it into the fire, and out came this calf,"* Ex 32:24). We might blame others, like Adam (*"the woman whom you gave to be with me, she gave me fruit of the tree, and I ate,"* Gen 3:12). The methods differ, but the record of Scripture tells us emphatically that we are extremely likely to try to conceal our sins.

The other path is for *"he who confesses and forsakes"* sin. Psalm 51 is the record of how David pours out his heart before God because of this sin. He confesses freely (Psalm 51:4, 9, 14). He grieves his sin and begs for mercy. *"The sacrifices of God are a broken spirit; a broken and contrite heart, O God, you will not despise"*(Psalm 51:17). There is no concealing—and no pride—in a broken and contrite heart.

It is not just David. Even wicked King Ahab, challenged by the prophet Elijah about his murder of Naboth, humbles himself and admits his sin. He *"tore his clothes and put sackcloth on his flesh and fasted and lay in sackcloth and went about dejectedly"*(1 Kings 21:27). His behavior is so impressive that God himself comments that *"he has humbled himself before me"*(1 Kings 21:29). Humility comes when we stop pretending that everything is normal and own our sin.

John also describes two possible options when we sin. *"If we say we have no sin"*—this is the denial option—*"we deceive ourselves, and the truth is not in us. If we confess our sins"*—this is the confession and forsaking option—*"he is faithful and just to forgive us our sins and to cleanse us from all unrighteousness"*(1 John 1:8-9). While John is focusing on confession to God rather than people, the essential principle is the same: we have a vital choice to make every time we discover we have done wrong in any way. We will be tempted to hide our sin and justify ourselves. But mercy is for those who confess their sins.

James tells Christians to *"confess your sins to one another and pray for one another, that you may be healed. The prayer of a righteous person has great power as it is working"* (James 5:16). Christians will sin. This is about the right response to sin. We do not hide it or pretend that we have not sinned. We confess and ask others to pray for our forgiveness and healing.

Why Is This Hard?

This last passage is one of the most neglected in Scripture. The difficulty here is not in understanding the verse, which is rather plain. The challenge is that confessing our sins to others is humiliating. It makes us vulnerable to them. We risk losing their respect. It scares us because some people (yes, even Christians) are not trustworthy and may spread our confession around. James is not saying that we have to confess *every* sin to *everyone* we know. He is not telling us to make a public confession of sin in the assembly or to a priest (neither of these practices is described in the New Testament). He is teaching us about the power that comes from humbling ourselves, opening up our hearts to our brothers and sisters, and interceding before God for one another. That's hard.

Confessing sins is a challenge because we are often engaged in image management. We want people to like us and think well of us. One of the best ways to accomplish this is to limit the information they have about us. If we can always put our best foot forward, we can look a lot better than we are. Yet if we confess our sins, we deliberately expose to others our most shameful secrets. We turn that entire process upside-down.

It is also <u>painful to relive our worst moments</u>. We are deeply embarrassed and ashamed of the evils we have committed. They hurt. So discussing them with others—especially when they are fresh—is a profound challenge.

We can grow quite <u>stubborn in our refusal to confess</u> our sins. We make excuses for why we don't need to confess. Why does it matter anyway? Why do others need to know? I can deal with this on my own! In our pride, we insist that we can correct our sin in isolation, away from others who can help us and pray for us. We find fault with our brethren and assume they would judge us harshly. We wonder if our sin is just not really that big a deal. We bow up against passages that teach us to confess. We expend a great deal of energy insisting that we don't need to do what God tells us to.

Most of all, confession is difficult because <u>we worry that others won't love us if they really know us</u>. Whether that is our romantic partners, who might find the things we have done, said, and thought disgusting—or our friends, who might decide we aren't worth the trouble—or our family, who might embarrass or disown us—we fear the rejection that comes from revealing our sins.

How Does This Help with Humility?

Confessing sins <u>dispels our pretenses at perfection</u>. We are not perfect—not even close—and we cannot pretend that we are as we reveal our sins and weaknesses. This lowers us.

Confession reminds us that <u>we are not above the law</u>. God condemns in me the same things he condemns in others. Instead, we open ourselves up, admitting our weaknesses and inviting criticism. When we sin, *we have a problem*. Those who love us can help us solve it. We make ourselves accountable to those who can strengthen us to grow and improve.

There is also something liberating about confessing to our brothers and sisters. <u>We don't have to hide anymore</u>. We can deal with the real issues we are struggling with. We can talk about them. And we always discover that others wrestle with the same things. We encourage each other, correct each other, and pray together. We are not above others, but on the same plane.

Confessing our sins also <u>reminds us that we need others</u>. The gospel thrives in communities because we sharpen one another and help each other draw closer to Jesus. God does not intend us to follow Jesus alone. It is humbling to remember that we need others to encourage and help us.

Practice humility. Find a Christian you trust and confess a sin. Fill them in on what your greatest struggles are. Talk to them about how you need help and prayer and accountability.

Practice humility. Confess a sin.

Field Notes

- <u>Not everyone is worthy of your secrets</u>. Learning to confess sins to others requires judgment about the trustworthiness and disposition of others. If others have evidenced a strongly judgmental spirit—or we know that they have struggled to love others who have confessed sin in the past—then we may not find them to be the kind of "confess and pray" partner we are seeking.

- <u>We have to be close to people to be willing to confess to them</u>. In most situations, I struggle baring my soul to people who don't know me well. The danger is that in times of spiritual struggle, we tend to pull away from others. We don't feel close to them and may even blame them for the disconnect. But I have also been guilty of waiting for the perfect friend and mentor before I would confess to someone. It may be that we just have to find someone we are somewhat close to and take the risk.

CHAPTER 2: PRAY FOR SOMEONE

I T IS EASY FOR US TO BECOME SELF-ABSORBED. We naturally take care of our own needs and solve our own problems. But we may take this too far. We can fail to notice that our relationships have become primarily about our validation. We can grow overly fascinated with our own thoughts and experiences. When this happens, where is the room for serious consideration of others and their needs and desires?

Of course, this fixation can corrupt our service to God. Our spiritual work and prayer lives become merely about God and us. We can neglect the vital role God intends others to play in our service and maturity.

Humility comes when we pray for someone else.

The Biblical Connection

Prayer is primarily a conversation between an individual and God. Yet very early on in the Bible, servants of God begin to use their relationship with God to request favors for others. Abraham intercedes for Sodom (Gen 18:23-33) and Moses attempts to intercede for Israel (Ex 32:30-34). They are praying, yet they are not praying for themselves. This kind of intercessory prayer contains a rare blend of boldness (to approach God and ask him to change his will) and humility (because we are asking these blessings for others).

In the New Testament, Paul regularly prays for new Christians that he has converted or heard about. "*And so, from the day we heard, we have not ceased to pray for you, asking that you may be filled with the knowledge of his will in all spiritual wisdom and understanding, so as to walk in a manner worthy of the Lord, fully pleasing to him, bearing fruit in every good work and increasing in the knowledge of God*"(Col 1:9-10). Paul's prayer is not casual. He has thought deeply about the Colossians (despite not knowing them personally, Col 2:1) and their spiritual needs. He expresses that thought in prayer.

He also mentions that Epaphras—who probably converted most of the Colossian Christians (Col 1:7)—is busy praying for them. "*Epaphras, who is one of you, a servant of Christ Jesus, greets you, always struggling on your behalf in his prayers, that you may stand mature and fully assured in all the will of God*"(Col 4:12). Epaphras is wrestling and struggling to win a blessing for the Colossians, continually asking for God to help them grow.

The prayers of Paul and Epaphras are focused on the spiritual development of the Colossians. They do not pray for their lives to be free from trouble. They do not pray for the churches to grow in number. They ask God for specific help in supplementing areas of spiritual weakness so that they can more fully realize the power of God and the transformation he brings. This is profoundly selfless prayer.

Paul also asks the Colossians to make *him* the subject of *their* prayers. *"At the same time, pray also for us, that God may open to us a door for the word, to declare the mystery of Christ, on account of which I am in prison—that I may make it clear, which is how I ought to speak"*(Col 4:3-4). He opens up about his concerns and needs. He longs for opportunities to teach the gospel and seeks God's help in his efforts to make the truth as clear as possible.

People who have a connection with God show their faith in him and love for others by praying for more than themselves.

Why Is This Hard?

Praying for others is hard when <u>we are more focused on our own needs and concerns</u>. We pray about our day, how we are feeling, what we would like to accomplish. We express our gratitude. We constantly think about what we need and what we want. Our prayers naturally center around ourselves—which makes praying for others *un*natural.

Some of that is understandable because prayer is deeply personal. When Jesus teaches his disciples to pray, there is almost no mention of others. He instructs them to pray honor to the Father, for the kingdom to come, for daily bread, for forgiveness, and for deliverance from evil and temptation. Even when others do figure into the prayer (*"as we also have forgiven our debtors,"* Matt 6:12), it is in connection with our own forgiveness. So it is natural that disciples of Jesus may fix the attention of their prayers primarily on their own relationships with God. But Jesus does not neglect others in his personal prayers. He tells the disciples to pray for God to send laborers into the harvest (Matt 9:38). He prays for

Peter's faith not to fail (Luke 22:32). He prays at length for the sanctification of the eleven and the unity of all believers (John 17:6–26). Jesus shows us that <u>an intense prayer life involves a balance of praying for ourselves and others</u>. That balance is hard to strike perfectly.

Praying for others is hard because <u>their worries and crises are not naturally as prominent in our thinking</u>. We don't always feel their pain the way we feel our own. We may grieve with them momentarily—or show deep concern for them for a little while—yet we eventually return to our default concern for ourselves. We struggle to continually remind ourselves to pray for others and their needs.

Praying for others <u>requires deep thought about what would be *best* for them</u>. We pray primarily in times of crisis—whether for ourselves or others. We are more likely to pray for others when we hear that someone is in the hospital or facing unemployment. Yet there is no pressing crisis that prompts Paul's prayers. He shows a concern for the *spiritual maturity* of these Christians in ordinary circumstances. They are always on his mind. He is continually aware of where they are spiritually and where they need to go. This kind of focus must be learned.

How Does This Help with Humility?

In intercessory prayer, we are <u>leveraging our relationship with God *not for our own good, but for the good of someone else*</u>. Nothing in this process directly involves us—and that's the point. It's not about us. We ask a blessing simply for the good of the person we want God to bless. Praying for others helps us resist the temptation to saturate our prayers with our own concerns about comfort and pleasure. Just for a little while, we can approach God's throne and say: "I'm not here for me today." When we pray for someone, we enter into their world. We think about their needs, growth, hopes, and fears. We consider more than just how they affect us or reflect on us. We finally—if only for a moment—get ourselves out of the way and do something to help others.

Paul instructs the Philippians to "*do nothing from selfish ambition or conceit, but in humility count others more significant than yourselves. Let each of you look not only to his own interests, but also to the interests of others*"(Phil 2:3-4). Humility necessitates <u>looking out for the interests of others</u>, not just our own. If we count others as more significant than ourselves, this will require thought and effort.

Instead of simply unloading whatever is on our minds, we begin to think carefully about the concerns and needs others have. Who do we know that is in need? What could we request from God on their behalf? Then we grow a level deeper: What needs do they have that are not readily apparent? How can they grow spiritually? What is God's will for them? And we pray: "Father, help this brother grow into a stronger father so that he can lead his children to their Father. Work in him to learn and grow so that he can also lead your people in a local church. Develop his character so that others can see you are at work in him and he can lead lost people to you." And we pray: "Father, watch over this sister as she battles the challenges of old age. Keep her mind and spirit sharp. Strengthen her to remain connected to you. Empower her to teach others from her reservoir of Bible knowledge and life experience. Make her an example of faithful service through the final stages of life." When we pray like this, our personal concerns fade into the background.

More, we can pray with the confidence that God looks favorably on such prayers. When Abraham approaches God on behalf of Sodom, he pleads for mercy on behalf of Lot and whatever other righteous people might be living in the city (Gen 18:23-24). This request is audacious. He is asking God to change his will simply because he is asking. Yet God not only allows such prayer; he answers favorably. Even though he ultimately destroys the city, *"God remembered Abraham and sent Lot out of the midst of the overthrow"*(Gen 19:29). Intercession works.

Practice humility. Think deeply about someone else's needs—particularly their spiritual needs—and pray for them.

Field Notes

- <u>Pray through your circles</u>. If at a loss for where to start, I have found it helpful to pray for different sets of people. I can go through my family one by one. Sometimes I mentally travel around our church building, thinking of the people who sit in a certain pew and pondering what their needs and struggles are. Work through your close friends or your workplace acquaintances. Take time with each person. What is it like to be them? What are their anxieties and hurts? What are their great strengths? What spiritual needs do they have?

- <u>See them like God sees them</u>. Praying for others is easier when I have a clear vision of a person's talents and gifts, struggles and concerns. The more I know about them, the better I pray. Yet I have to think of them in the way God does—not only concerned about how they affect me, but focused on a higher purpose for their lives. Then when I see a need—for someone to take a stronger role of leadership, for a brother to overcome an anger problem—I can pray confidently that it is God's will too.

CHAPTER 3: ADMIT YOU DON'T KNOW

N O ONE LIKES TO APPEAR UNINFORMED. Yet all of us have both our areas of expertise and subjects about which we know very little—either from a lack of experience, schooling, or thought. The temptation is to bridge that gap by pretending and blustering, trying to convince others that we are more knowledgeable than we are.

Humility comes when we are willing to admit our ignorance.

The Biblical Connection

Paul is concerned about knowledge causing problems in Corinth. The issue is that animals that have been ceremonially offered to a false god (like Zeus) are then slaughtered and sold in the meat market in Corinth. Should Christians eat it? One group is hesitant for reasons of conscience: they feel it would be honoring that false god. Another is comfortable because of their knowledge: they know that these gods are not real.

So Paul addresses the issue: "*Now concerning food offered to idols: we know that 'all of us possess knowledge.' This 'knowledge' puffs up, but* love builds up. If anyone imagines that he knows something, he does not yet know as he ought to know. But if anyone loves God, he is known by God"(1 Cor 8:1-3). Paul connects knowledge to pride ("knowledge puffs up, but love builds up"). Very often we think that knowing things—especially knowing more than someone else—makes us better than others. We cannot understand why they don't get it. Paul insists that true knowledge if found in admitting that we don't know: "If anyone imagines that he knows something, he does not yet know as he ought to know."

He gives this caution: "If anyone among you thinks that he is wise in this age, let him become a fool that he may become wise"(1 Cor 3:18). If we are "know-it-alls," either we truly know it all or we are proud and delusional. Both of those options are distasteful; better to "become a fool" by admitting we don't know.

The stated intent of the book of Proverbs is "to give prudence to the simple, knowledge and discretion to the youth"(Prov 1:4). The path toward true wisdom comes with the acknowledgement that we have blind spots and need help seeing ourselves—and the world—rightly. We begin to learn when we see how much we need to learn.

Scripture also repeatedly informs us that there are limits to our knowledge. "The secret things belong to the LORD our God, but the things that are revealed belong to us and to our children forever, that we may do all the words of this law"(Deut 29:29). Some knowledge—especially about God and the way he runs his world—is outside our purview. God confronts Job by asking him, "Who is this that darkens counsel by words without knowledge?"(Job 38:2). When he is finally chastened, Job admits, "I have uttered what I did not understand, things too wonderful for me, which I did not know"(Job 42:3). David even describes some truths that are too grand for full human comprehension. As he contemplates God's complete knowledge of him, he declares that "*such knowledge is too wonderful for me; it is high; I cannot attain it*" (Psalm 139:6).

When we admit our ignorance, we join a long line of faithful servants of God.

Why Is This Hard?

Admitting we don't know is hard because <u>we are afraid we will lose the esteem of others</u>. When I first began preaching, I believed that I had to act as if I knew and understood everything. I needed to answer every question, explain every passage, and grasp every concept. I was afraid that if I ever admitted I didn't know something, I would lose respect. What good is a preacher who doesn't know? Of course, this led to embarrassing situations where I would pretend to know something that I didn't. Surprisingly, I have found that people often appreciate the honesty of admitting that I haven't thought about certain things, don't fully understand, and cannot satisfactorily explain parts of the faith. There is freedom here.

In many areas, <u>ignorance is mistaken for incompetence</u>. By admitting we don't know, we fear that we will not only lose respect, but lose out on future career opportunities or chances to influence others. If we don't know this, what *do* we know? Why would people call on us to help them if we don't know anything?

There is a <u>social pressure to pretend we know things</u> as well. When everyone around us knows something—or acts as if they do—then we feel a pressure to fit in. Displaying our ignorance might mean that others mock and laugh at us. They might exclude us if we don't have something meaningful to add. Most of all, we just won't look as good in front of others.

Owning our ignorance means that <u>we are displaying our weakness, insufficiency, and limitations</u>. It can seem humiliating to show others how we come up short. We are trained from a young age to hide our weaknesses. Admitting that we don't know highlights our shortcomings for all to see.

How Does This Help with Humility?

Each time we admit we don't know, we lower ourselves. <u>We have confessed our inadequacy</u>. We no longer have to impress others and be an expert on every topic. We are free to learn and listen to others. Perhaps they have insights and knowledge that will bless us. There is no need to look down on others—and if they decide to look down on us, then that is *their* failing.

Admitting we don't know <u>elevates others</u>. We all have our own areas of knowledge and areas of ignorance. Can we let others have a moment to shine? This is a way of humbling ourselves before God (who knows all) and others (who know more than I do in many areas).

David summarizes the <u>liberating peace</u> this brings: "*O LORD, my heart is not lifted up; my eyes are not raised too high; I do not occupy myself with things too great and too marvelous for me. But I have calmed and quieted my soul, like a weaned child with its mother; like a weaned child is my soul within me*"(Psalm 131:1-2). David admits that there are things "*too great and marvelous for me,*" but he does not worry about it. This is true for all of us; it is just that David acknowledges it. There are some things he doesn't know. This doesn't keep him up at night, though. He is still content and calm.

Practice humility. Take every opportunity to admit you don't know.

Field Notes

- <u>Distinguish between things that are within your expertise and those that are not</u>. As I implemented this practice, I received a Bible question that I was able to answer quickly in a text message. Shortly afterward, I received a phone call with a matter regarding parental judgment, day care, and physical safety. I was at a loss—and I said so. There was a dramatic difference in the way I felt when something was within my expertise (confident) and when something was not (confused, uncertain). This practice gives voice to that emotion.

- <u>Admitting we don't know is not merely a part of a self-deprecating personality</u>. Sometimes we deliberately insult ourselves ("I don't know much" or "I'm not that smart, but..") to come across better. The practice of admitting we don't know is not a general approach to life, but needs specific expression in a situation. "I don't know how to help you" or "I don't know how to answer that" are much closer to the intent here.

CHAPTER 4: SKIP A MEAL

HUMILITY IS CHALLENGING TO THOSE WHO expect to always have everything they want immediately. In this mentality, our desires are in charge and must be met. We easily become convinced that we *deserve* these blessings. They are basic and we are entitled to them. It would be shocking to *not* have what we want.

An effective way to challenge this mentality is to force ourselves to do without. Skip a meal.

The Biblical Connection

The Bible connects humility and fasting. Ezra describes his actions as he prepares to cross the desert from Persia to Jerusalem: *"Then I proclaimed a fast there, at the river Ahava, that we might humble ourselves before our God, to seek from him a safe journey for ourselves, our children, and all our goods"*(Ezra 8:21). A fast helps them *"humble ourselves before our God."*

In fact, Scripture sometimes treats fasting and humility as synonyms. One leads to the other. *"Why have we fasted, and you see it not? Why have we humbled ourselves, and you take no knowledge?"*(Isa 58:3). In response, God asks, *"Is such the fast that I choose, a day for a person to humble himself?"*(Isa 58:5). God is pushing them to do more than just fasting, yet in doing so, he describes fasting as humility.

Fasting indicates that all is not well. Like Ezra (and many others in Scripture), we go without food to seek God's help. Or like Nehemiah (and many others in Scripture), we go without food to mourn our sin. Whatever the motivation, it is *not* business as usual. And in both cases fasting is a way we express our need for God.

But even regular fasts are about humbling ourselves to focus on honoring God. When Jesus teaches his disciples about their fasting, he emphasizes this connection: *"And when you fast, do not look gloomy like the hypocrites, for they disfigure their faces that their fasting may be seen by others. Truly, I say to you, they have received their reward. But when you fast, anoint your head and wash your face, that your fasting may not be seen by others but by your Father who is in secret. And your Father who sees in secret will reward you"*(Matt 6:16-18). This kind of fasting does not have a special need behind it. It is a fast to simply honor God and focus our attention on him.

Why Is This Hard?

Fasting is hard because <u>we like to eat</u>. We develop habits of eating at certain times—whether we are hungry or not—and those habits are hard to challenge. Most Americans have grown accustomed to having their favorite foods ready for them at a moment's notice. We have fresh fruit year-round. Every day has its own gourmet experience. There is eerie similarity to the rich man in Jesus' story who *"feasted sumptuously every day"*(Luke 16:19). Our constant stream of food makes it easy for us to forget that much of the world lives in legitimate hunger. We become so accustomed to these pleasures that we scarcely register them— unless we don't have them.

Of course, <u>fasting is also uncomfortable</u>. We will experience hunger pangs. We get fussy. There may be headaches. We will have to volunteer for something unpleasant in pursuit of something deeper.

Skipping meals is also <u>not culturally acceptable</u>. The only times fasting is practiced without criticism in modern America are when we are working or dieting. This means that if we willingly fast, people will notice, bother us, try to dissuade us, or just generally call attention to us. They will think that we are weird.

That response even occurs among Christians. <u>Many Christians argue that Christians should not fast</u>. This is surprising, given Jesus' instructions to his disciples on the topic (Matt 6:16-18) and his promise that his disciples will fast after he is gone (Matt 9:15). In describing the church in Antioch—a group of Christians—Luke tells us that "*while they were worshiping the Lord and fasting, the Holy Spirit said, 'Set apart for me Barnabas and Saul for the work to which I have called them.' Then after fasting and praying they laid their hands on them and sent them off*"(Acts 13:2-3). Their regular fasting is interrupted by a special message from the Spirit, after which they hold a special fast (presumably to ask God's blessing on their journey). Fasting is a Christian practice.

Despite these biblical instructions, <u>fasting seems rare</u>, even among Christians. Most Christians just don't talk about it—or do so just long enough to laugh at the absurdity of the thought.

Fasting is hard because we often not only have to fight our own cravings, but the criticism of fellow-disciples.

We are also challenged by the fact that <u>we don't like to deny ourselves things that we're not *required* to</u>. There is no specific command by which we know that we *must* fast, so we struggle to see the value in it. If we *can* eat whenever we choose, why *wouldn't* we? This mentality is hard to shake. Its very optional nature means we often just opt out. And what kind of disciple is that?

How Does This Help with Humility?

Fasting humbles us because it <u>breaks our insistence that we always have everything we want (or even everything we need)</u>. Skipping a meal reminds us that there are more important things than our comfort and satisfaction. There are times when appealing to God, expressing regret to God, or simply focusing on him are so important that other things must be pushed aside. Our needs are not the most important thing. Our hunger can take a backseat to the spiritual priorities of our lives.

Fasting <u>helps us to regain control over our impulses</u>. One of the biggest problems in modern America is our inability to deny ourselves and take care of our bodies. Even when we know we shouldn't eat or do something, we are often powerless to stop ourselves. We become slaves of the body and its desires. If anyone should be leading the way in changing and fighting against this slavery, it is Christians. Yet instead, we gain weight and our habits contribute to our health problems. We lack the self-discipline to say no to the simplest impulses for even short amounts of time. But when someone challenges us to fast, we object strenuously.

There is pride here. Fasting reminds us of God's expectation that we control our bodies in holiness and honor (1 Thess 4:4).

Fasting <u>reminds us that full bellies are not our natural state</u>. Throughout history, hunger has always been more common that fullness, discomfort more common than ease, pain more common than pleasure. We easily get used to our blessings and become petulant when deprived of them. We blame our bad moods, short tempers, and ugly words on our hunger. Fasting restores order here. If we cannot treat others well while hungry, perhaps it is not the food that is the problem. As we grow more aware of our own character flaws and more grateful for God's provision, we grow more humble.

God and his purposes are the most important thing. *Why is it that God's things are sometimes neglected while my eating <u>never</u> is?*

Practice humility. Skip a meal and use that time and energy to focus on God.

Field Notes

- <u>Start small</u>. You don't have to fast for 40 days. Start by skipping a meal.

- <u>Fasting should be active</u>. Use the time you would have spent eating to focus on God's word, prayer, and spiritual awareness. When you get hungry, say a prayer.

- <u>You may be more used to eating than you realize</u>. In my fasting I have often found myself mindlessly gravitating toward eating. While doing something else, I will get up to go get some food before I realize what I am doing. This surprised me and convicted me that for me there is almost no intermediate state between hunger and instant gratification.

- <u>Prepare for people to ruin your fasting!</u> When I began to attempt fasting, people seemed to ask me more about my eating and invited me out to eat more!

- <u>Work on your mood</u>. Many people get cranky when they don't eat. Knowing that we are doing without should be accompanied with strong effort to be pleasant. We don't want those close to us to dread our efforts to draw closer to God.

CHAPTER 5: READ THE BIBLE FOR NO REASON

F ROM A YOUNG AGE, WE ARE ENCOURAGED to believe that we are independent and self-sustaining. We so emphasize our role in providing for ourselves, accomplishing our goals, and taking care of our business that we unwittingly grow arrogant. Yet God assures us that not only is he the source of good things in our lives (James 1:17), but that we also need him on a regular basis to renew our thinking (Eph 4:23).

We need to hear from God. This is different from needing God to provide arguments for us to win religious debates. As C.S. Lewis said, "A man can't always be defending the truth; there must be a time to feed on it."[5]

Read the Bible—not to study a certain book or to prove someone wrong or to check a box. Read the Bible for no reason—except to know God better.

---

[5] Lewis, *Reflections on the Psalms*, p. 8.

The Biblical Connection

When Satan tempts Jesus to turn stones into bread, he answers by quoting from Deuteronomy. *"It is written, 'Man shall not live by bread alone, but by every word that comes from the mouth of God'"*(Matt 4:4). As often happens with Jesus, his answer works on multiple levels. He quotes Scripture, which implies a rich familiarity with what is in the Bible. But the Scripture he quotes also stresses the importance of Scripture. Man does not simply need bread to live. True life comes from absorbing and consuming the words of God. Scripture tells us that we need Scripture.

Jesus' familiarity with Scripture helps him resist temptation. David also speaks at length about his reliance on God's word in his daily life. *"Your testimonies are my delight; they are my counselors"*(Psalm 119:24). Or again, *"I have stored up your word in my heart, that I might not sin against you"*(Psalm 119:11). He longs to hear God's words again: *"I open my mouth and pant, because I long for your commandments"*(Psalm 119:131).

What Jesus and David model here is a hunger for the word of God as more than mere information. This is how we come to know God and use his wisdom to navigate our lives. God's word is a source of spiritual life for us. We do not live by bread alone, but by God's word. We read so that we can re-enter the world steeped in God's thinking and nourished by his truth.

The Bible helps us to know ourselves. James likens the word to a mirror (James 1:22-25) that shows us precisely as we are. Paul warns the Romans, *"Do not be conformed to this world, but be transformed by the renewal of your mind, that by testing you may discern what is the will of God, what is good and acceptable and perfect"*(Rom

12:1). While Paul does not specify how we renew our minds, he connects the renewal with "*the will of God.*" By hearing from God, our perspectives are recalibrated and refreshed. The Bible helps us to be renewed. The Bible tells us about the heart of God (1 Tim 2:3-4) and his will for the world (Col 1:19-20). *These are not phenomena that occur only in a structured study course. They permeate the Bible. They are gained by consistent reading.*

This is why Paul encourages Timothy to give his attention to the "*sacred writings*"(what we call the Old Testament) because "*all Scripture is breathed out by God and profitable for teaching, for reproof, for correction, and for training in righteousness, that the man of God may be complete, equipped for every good work*"(2 Tim 3:16-17). He stresses that *all* Scripture is profitable to teach us things that will bless us in everyday living. Certainly there are some parts of the Bible that are more accessible than others, but everything God gives us is useful for us.

Reading the Bible for no reason will help us experience a sense of dependence. We approach the Bible not to master a set of facts or to pursue an agenda. We simply seek to know God more deeply.

Why Is This Hard?

We often want a purpose or goal in our Bible reading. Of course this can be good. There are times when we need to work through a particular subject. Sometimes we just want increased familiarity with the message of a certain book or passage. Reading plans can be helpful to make our study systematic. Yet <u>sometimes our systems, goals, and plans get in the way of our reading</u>. We pursue our goals instead of simply hearing God's voice in the word. Also, people have often told me of the struggles, sense of failure, and mindless reading that accompany some Bible reading plans. This all contributes to a sense of difficulty in regular Bible study.

Reading the Bible is challenging for us because the Bible <u>often seems outdated</u>. Perhaps that is because we are already familiar with the text to the degree that we struggle to see any freshness in the reading. Perhaps it is because its connection to a bygone era makes it seem irrelevant to modern times and problems. These feelings add an extra layer of challenge because we must expend a lot of energy to pull something out of the Bible.

We struggle reading the Bible generally because <u>we are busy with other things</u>. We have our responsibilities in different arenas of life. When we set those down for a few minutes, we often long for pleasant distractions or entertainment. The Bible is not really a distraction or particularly entertaining. In fact, the difficulty we encounter in applying the Bible to our lives often feels like more work of a different kind.

Most of all, reading the Bible without a clear agenda is hard because *we don't think we need it*. While Christians agree that the Bible is important, we are not deeply convicted that we need Scripture to renew our minds, to draw us closer to God, to help us make decisions, to mature our perspectives, to give moral courage, and to teach us how to treat others.

In other words, reading the Bible is hard because of our preoccupation with our own goals and our feeling that the Bible won't really help us achieve them.

How Does This Help with Humility?

Focusing this way on Scripture—where we come to the Bible to learn about God—<u>reminds us that we are not the center of the universe</u>. God's story involves many people and a long period of time in many different places. He has done so much for all people that suddenly our concerns about our car breaking down or what our coworker said to us are completely unimportant by comparison. There is a bigger story going on than ours.

If we approach Scripture with personal agendas, our study often leaves us prouder. We want to prove someone else wrong. We want to condemn their behavior. We want to out-argue them. We want to justify ourselves or our group or our family. We want to grasp things on a different level and then champion our own enlightenment. Yet if we leave Scripture prouder than we came, we are reading it wrong. Reading the Bible for no reason leaves us free to listen to what God wants to say and go where he wants to lead us. We gaze in wonder at the works of God and ask with David, "What is man?"(Psalm 8). We watch in awe as God divides the Red Sea or rebuilds the walls of Jerusalem. We marvel at Jesus' prayer for his crucifiers, "Father, forgive them." These are not sermons to be preached or arguments to be marshalled. We see ourselves in these stories, but not as the heroes. <u>Read properly, the Bible always leaves us humbled</u>.

Reading the Bible reminds us that <u>we are dependent on God</u>. We are insufficient on our own. We need correction, recalibration, and renewal. We tend to get into ruts of thinking. We tend to be overly influenced by our culture. We tend to navel-gaze. We assume that we are right and others are wrong. Scripture opens our eyes to our need for wisdom and help. Man does not live by bread alone, but by the word of God.

Particularly, reading the Bible *for no reason* helps us here. We do not approach the Bible attempting to master anything. We are not here to pursue our own expertise. We are not here to teach, but to learn. We are hungry and have come to eat. We want to put good things before our eyes. We want to renew our thinking. We want to be reminded of what we already know. We need positivity. We need refreshing where we have grown stale.

Read the Bible for no reason. Read a little bit and chew on it, thinking about what it reveals about God—or life—or you. Find out what you need to about the context or the meaning of difficult words—not to become an expert, but just to understand the meaning. Over the course of a few weeks of reading this way, you may find that your day is influenced by these thoughts and efforts. If you miss a day, you may find that you miss it—the way you would miss eating.

Practice humility. Read the Bible for no reason.

Field Notes

- <u>This is challenging for me because of my work.</u> Those of us who preach struggle reading the Bible for no reason. I naturally sketch sermons out of a text and think of what I could title it. I begin to think of all the applications I could make to other people and what it could do for our church. Sadly, for me, time spent in the Bible with nothing to show for it seems unproductive. Reading simply to be nourished will force us to quiet our minds and listen.

- <u>Reading the Bible for no reason feels aimless, but is really about *thinking through* a text</u>. We must do more than read—or even plan lessons. The goal here is renewing our thinking along biblical lines. How have I seen this principle? When have I experienced this emotion? In what ways have I been guilty? How does this challenge me? Questions like these help a text come to life.

CHAPTER 6: TAKE THE LOWEST PLACE

WE SEEK HONOR. Usually we feel upset when others do not give us the amount of respect we feel we deserve. We may feel compelled to insist on it. Occasionally we will even tell others all the reasons we are worthy of such esteem. We are undeterred by the fact that this often sabotages our efforts and torpedoes our relationships. After all, we *deserve* respect!

Humility takes a different approach to the problem of honor. Take the lowest place.

The Biblical Connection

The picture comes from Jesus. When invited to dinner, he observes the Jews around him scrambling to have the best places to sit—a key indicator of honor in that time.

> *"Now he told a parable to those who were invited, when he noticed how they chose the places of honor, saying to them, 'When you are invited by someone to a wedding feast, do not sit down in a place of honor, lest someone more distinguished than you be invited by him, and he*

who invited you both will come and say to you, "Give your place to this person," and then you will begin with shame to take the lowest place. But when you are invited, go and sit in the lowest place, so that when your host comes he may say to you, "Friend, move up higher." Then you will be honored in the presence of all who sit at table with you. For everyone who exalts himself will be humbled, and he who humbles himself will be exalted"(Luke 14:7-11).

Jesus advises them not to sit down in a place of honor. There is the risk that your host will not think you worthy of as much honor as you do. He may demote you. Jesus is warning us that we should not *assume* honor. He is also saying that we should not take honor *for ourselves*. We do not *insist* on honor. The reason is that *honor is given but can never be taken.*

The Proverbs stress that humility comes *before* honor. The order is important.

- *"The fear of the LORD is instruction in wisdom, and humility comes before honor"*(Prov 15:33).

- *"Before destruction a man's heart is haughty, but humility comes before honor"*(Prov 18:12).

- *"One's pride will bring him low, but he who is lowly in spirit will obtain honor"*(Prov 29:23).

When we get into honor-seeking mode, we also struggle with watching others receive honor. Whatever honor they receive, we feel they don't deserve (or at least not as much as we do). The classic biblical example here is Haman, a prominent royal official in ancient Persia. He has a feud with a Jew named Mordecai. The king asks Haman what should be done for someone the king wants to honor. In his arrogance, Haman assumes that he is the one the king will honor and has a ready list of all the gifts and praises that he would like. Yet when the king honors Mordecai this way, *"Haman hurried to his house, mourning and with his head covered"*(Esther 6:12). Haman's pursuit of honor leaves him humbled and shamed while Mordecai's humility is blessed by the king (and God).

Why Is This Hard?

We do want to be honored. We want to be shown and recognized as valuable and noteworthy. We often feel that others' respect validates us, our work, and our choices. But the challenge in honor is that it is counterintuitive to seek something by *not* seeking it. It is hard for us to lower ourselves and trust that someday, somehow, at some point, we will be honored. It is much more natural for us to seek honor for ourselves.

Taking the lowest place is hard because it requires faith. We trust that even if others never grasp our worth, God does and will exalt us when he is ready. *"For everyone who exalts himself will be humbled, and he who humbles himself will be exalted."* This a promise in the future tense—*"everyone who exalts himself will be humbled"*. Jesus assures us that God will do the honoring, but that can be hard to believe.

It also seems (to me, at least) that this is a case where there is a conflict between what we *want* to happen and what we really believe _will_ happen. We want the world to work in a way where the humble are honored and the arrogant are humiliated, yet we know that we don't always see this happen. Instead, we very often see the proud blessed and rewarded for their arrogance. They bluster and assert themselves and take the best seats and insist on the honor of men—_and they receive it._ We are tempted to take Jesus' words as nice platitudes, all the while believing that it's not really the way the world works.

Taking the lowest place is a decisive step toward trusting God.

How Does This Help with Humility?

Taking the lowest place means that <u>we lower ourselves before others</u>—not as a ploy, but because we refuse to assume that we deserve honor. We give up on seeking honor. We are fully content with however we end up—honored by the host or eating the full meal in the lowest place.

By taking the lowest place, <u>we don't insist on special treatment, titles, and signs of respect</u>. Like Peter, we may even flat-out refuse such honors: "_Stand up; I too am a man_"(Acts 10:26). Like Daniel, we may brush aside empty flattery: "_Let your gifts be for yourself, and give your rewards to another_"(Dan 5:17). Whatever the case, taking the lowest place means that we view ourselves—and present ourselves to others—as ordinary people.

By taking the lowest place, <u>we do the right thing whether others notice or not</u>. Our lives are lived before the audience of God, not other men. We do not await their praise. If they notice the life we are living in service to God and approve, that is fine. But we are faithful regardless.

By taking the lowest place, we *"let another praise you, and not your own mouth; a stranger, and not your own lips"*(Prov 27:2). We do not need to tell others about our greatness. We let others decide what they think about us; our goal is simply to live rightly.

By taking the lowest place, <u>we sit, work, and live in obscurity— and don't worry about it</u>.

Practice humility. Let others go before you, sit above you, hog the conversation, brag about themselves, and ignore or denigrate you. Take the lowest place.

Field Notes

- <u>Prepare for others to take the low road when you take the high road</u>. The fact that we try to do the right thing doesn't mean others will do the same. In fact, they will likely try to take advantage of the fact that we do not assert ourselves, treating it as a kind of weakness. It is important to be prepared for the emotional shock of this. Not everyone will support our refusal to seek honor.

- <u>It is hard to watch others get attention—even when you know better</u>. I have occasionally made decisions that I know will limit my public exposure and honor. Yet even when I am the one who makes the decision—and I do it from pure motives—I have been surprised by the difficulty I have in seeing others be honored ahead of and before me. This is the role to which Jesus is calling us.

CHAPTER 7: CONSIDER THE OTHER SIDE

ALL PEOPLE TEND TO THINK that they are right. Our thoughts, opinions, plans, and conclusions seem axiomatically correct. This often leads to pride. We have little patience for the perspective of others. We don't like to consider the possibility that we are wrong. We refuse to even listen.

Humility will require considering the other side.

The Biblical Connection

Luke tells us about how a preacher named Apollos gains a better understanding of the truth about Jesus from Aquila and Priscilla.

> "Now a Jew named Apollos, a native of Alexandria, came to Ephesus. He was an eloquent man, competent in the Scriptures. He had been instructed in the way of the Lord. And being fervent in spirit, he spoke and taught accurately the things concerning Jesus, though he knew only the baptism of John. He began to speak boldly in

the synagogue, but when Priscilla and Aquila heard him,
they took him aside and explained to him the way of God
more accurately"(Acts 18:24-26).

Apollos is eloquent, knowledgeable, and enthusiastic. People are already listening to him. All of these things would seem to work against him honestly considering this rebuke. There is more to the message of Jesus than what Apollos knows, but that doesn't mean that he's going to be willing to hear it. If Apollos were proud, his reaction would be far different. He might bristle at Aquila and Priscilla ("Who do you think you are?") or appeal to his own considerable gifts ("I can talk circles around you") or simply refuse to listen ("I know all I need to know"). Instead, Apollos is humble enough to listen to Aquila and Priscilla and becomes convinced that they are right. He now begins to preach about Jesus *"more accurately."*

We don't always take opposition as well as Apollos. Often we fail to even consider what others are saying. We start the interaction believing we are right and they are wrong. We barely listen. We are convinced that they have nothing meaningful to add to our (already correct) position. Apollos teaches us the transformative power truth can have when we honestly consider the viewpoints of others.

Luke also describes some Jews who listen to Paul as he tells them about Jesus. *"Now these Jews were more noble than those in Thessalonica; they received the word with all eagerness, examining the Scriptures daily to see if these things were so"*(Acts 17:11). They do not reject Paul out of hand. They consider what he is saying, then examine the Scriptures to see if he's right. These Bereans have the humility not to assume that they are the arbiters of right and wrong. They consider Paul and examine Scripture. It is not surprising that *"many of them therefore believed"*(Acts 17:12).

The Bible also tells us about people who refuse to consider the other side. It happens in churches, where Diotrephes *"who likes to put himself first"* keeps *"talking wicked nonsense against us"* and *"refuses to welcome the brothers, and also stops those who want to and puts them out of the church"*(3 John 9-10). Diotrephes is not interested in honest discussion; he is too busy *"putting himself first."*

It happens in kingdoms, where young King Rehoboam deliberates over whether to lighten the load of taxation his father Solomon placed on the people. The older counselors encourage him to relax the burden, while the young men advise him to put his foot down. The text makes clear that he does not give honest consideration here: *"But he abandoned the counsel that the old men gave him and took counsel with the young men"*(1 Kings 12:8). Or even more directly: *"So the king did not listen to the people"*(1 Kings 12:15).

In each situation, refusal to consider the other side—and the possibility that we are wrong—is painted as an act of pride.

Why Is This Hard?

Considering the other side is difficult because <u>we think we are right</u>. We will have to suspend our defense of our perspective. We will likely have to be quiet. Very often we listen to others not to hear their arguments, but to rebut them. We want them to stop talking so that we can speak again. Humility means beginning with the possibility that we are wrong and stopping our tongues for a moment to truly consider the matter at hand.

Like Rehoboam, <u>sometimes we surround ourselves with like-minded people who share our perspective</u>. Where Rehoboam has a series of yes-man counselors, we have echo chambers where we repeat our beliefs to people who already agree with us. Often this merely leads to confirming what we already believed (and intensifying the belief). Social media algorithms present us with opinions and news items they know we already agree with. We may even isolate ourselves from people who have an opposing political or religious viewpoint, strengthening the "us vs. them" nature of the discussion. Considering the other side in modern times is not only intellectually and emotionally challenging; it has become hard to even *find* the people we disagree with.

Honestly considering others' opinions is hard because <u>it holds the unpleasant possibility that we are wrong</u>. The possibility exists not only that we have been wrong, but that we have been wrong for a long time. Major life-change might be necessary. We might have to take back things we have said and believed in the past. We might have to admit we don't know. We might have to defend a new belief. All of this makes us feel as if it is simpler to just continue on the course we are on. Why rock the boat? We're probably right anyway.

How Does This Help with Humility?

Considering the other side means that we must begin with the fact that we don't know everything (see chapter 3). But the deficiencies in our knowledge might lead to serious gaps and problems. What if we are wrong about something important? What if we make life-choices based on foolish or sinful thinking? <u>Listening well to others means that they may have the key to something that we have not considered</u>. We approach them with the spirit of a learner rather than a teacher. We lower ourselves before them.

This certainly doesn't mean that we must accept whatever we are told as if it were true. Ideas still must pass an evaluation process by which we determine their validity. It's just that if we never consider the other side, new ideas will never even reach the part of our minds where we honestly evaluate them. <u>When we consider the views of others, we move outside ourselves.</u> We get our egos out of the way, ready to think honestly, eager to learn.

There is another side in political issues, religious issues, and life issues. Why do others believe what they believe? Why do they think that way? What is appealing to them about their viewpoint? Do we understand what they are arguing? Could we explain their position in our own words? Do they have a point? Does it make sense? If we stood in their shoes, would we think like they do?

It may be that we consider what others believe and conclude that we are right. Yet this process will bless us by helping us believe more deeply and understand why it matters so much to us.

But it may be that we discover we have been wrong.

Practice humility. Consider the other side.

Field Notes

- <u>Considering the other side made me more frustrated when people did not listen to *me*</u>. As I tried to make improvements in my own open-mindedness, I found myself growing more exasperated when people did not pay me the same courtesy. They continued to treat me the way I had previously treated them—cutting me off, rushing to say their piece, assuming they had an answer before I had even stated my position. Intellectually I knew that I was the one trying to make changes (not them), but I still found it hard to stomach.

- <u>Often people are more open-minded than we expect</u>. As a preacher, people often assume they know what I think or how I would respond to a situation or idea. That frustrates me. Yet I often turn around and do the same to them—extrapolating from what I know about them to how they probably would react to a given thought. Yet when we give people a chance to listen and consider, they often surprise us. I have had this pleasant sensation in political matters as well as religious ones. It is a reminder that we are all more complex than we usually acknowledge.

CHAPTER 8: DISAGREE RESPECTFULLY

W E WILL DISAGREE WITH PEOPLE. We have our strong convictions about a host of topics, from sports to cats to religion. It is unlikely that we will find someone who agrees completely with us on any issue; it is impossible to find someone who sees our way on all of them.

Because we are convinced we are right, we often become arrogant in these situations. We feel that our job is not to listen (see chapter 7), but to instruct. We must show them how wrong they are. We must put them in their place. We must expose their ignorance.

Humility demands that we learn how to disagree respectfully.

The Biblical Connection

Paul, the veteran preacher, writes words of advice to young Timothy as he engages with others about spiritual things:

"Have nothing to do with foolish, ignorant controversies; you know that they breed quarrels. And the Lord's servant must not be quarrelsome but kind to everyone, able to teach, patiently enduring evil, correcting his opponents with gentleness. God may perhaps grant them repentance leading to a knowledge of the truth, and they may come to their senses and escape from the snare of the devil, after being captured by him to do his will"(2 Tim 2:23-26).

Some issues are to be avoided because *"they breed quarrels."* Not every discussion—religious or otherwise—is productive or important. We need discernment. Timothy should be *"kind"* and correct *"with gentleness."* This word is a synonym for humility. In fact, Paul adds a detailed, thoughtful description of the opponents Timothy will face: ensnared by Satan, out of their senses, and slaves. Such people deserve pity, not ridicule. Timothy will not agree with them, but he can temper his teaching with civility.

This passage teaches us to keep a careful watch on our own disposition, especially in controversy. We tend to get so worked up about the issue or argument that we forget to show respect to the *person*.

Peter also speaks about the difficulty of disagreeing with the right temperament. In the midst of hostility, he tells his readers to *"have no fear of them, nor be troubled, but in your hearts honor Christ the Lord as holy, always being prepared to make a defense to anyone who asks you for a reason for the hope that is in you; yet do it with gentleness and respect"*(1 Pet 3:14-15). We are not to be troubled or afraid of opposition, but to honor Christ in our hearts and be prepared to defend our hope. *"Yet do it with gentleness and respect."* The fact that others might be disrespectful doesn't mean we should. These verses anticipate conflict and fix our attitude for it: we will not always agree, but we can always be respectful.

When James speaks of the tongue, he warns us that *"with it we bless our Lord and Father, and with it we curse people who are made in the likeness of God"* (James 3:9). He reminds us that *all people are made in the likeness of God—even when they are wrong.*

We do not take our cues from the world. God instructs us in how we should think about the vital issues of life. But he also teaches us appropriate ways to interact with others about them. We *can* disagree respectfully.

Why Is This Hard?

When we disagree, we get so wrapped up in the *point*—the matter at hand—that <u>we become more concerned with being right than treating others well</u>. Sometimes we feel that we—like those in the passages above—are *defending God's truth* and convince ourselves that even courtesy means we are giving ground.

Often those who disagree with us aren't being very respectful either—so <u>we feel justified in fighting fire with fire</u>.

<u>Some forums—social media in particular—seem to discourage respectful dialogue</u>. Respect in such situations is a lot like trying to disarm a conflict while the crowd is chanting "Fight! Fight!" (think of elementary school students). People who see only one comment, post, or tweet suddenly begin the name-calling: Hitler, fascist,

socialist, stupid, or heretic. Respect is hard to give when it is not given.

   Past discussions play a role. If we have been poorly treated in the past, we can easily assume that the next disagreement will be as unpleasant as the last one and lash out preemptively. I have often replayed those old discussions in my mind again and again, dreaming up the ideal response. When the next opportunity arises, I think far more about my perfect answer than I do about the person I am speaking to and how I am treating them.

   Disagreeing respectfully is hard because we just tend to focus on either *ourselves* or the *content* of what we are trying to say. Humility is important here.

How Does This Help with Humility?

   These passages remind us of the personal side in any conflict. God calls us to gentleness and respect in these situations because he wants us to consider others as more than an opponent. We put ourselves in their shoes for just a moment. What would this look like from the other side of the discussion? Would we be likely to be convinced by someone who called us ugly names, talked over us, got disproportionately angry, and condescended to us? If we wouldn't like it, what makes us think it is justified or effective for us to do it to them?

   The priority of respect helps us to gain some critical distance from our actions. Some people (certainly never us!) are annoying and exasperating. Can we still respect them? Some people are misinformed, closed-minded, bigoted, hot-tempered, and corrupt. Can we still respect them? Our natural instinct is to assume that someone else's flaws justify our rough treatment of them. Yet Jesus reminds us that we are not only kind to those who are kind to us (Matt 5:46). Living these words is humility practice.

If we cannot be respectful in disagreeing about minor things—like politics, sports, personalities, science, or education—then what hope do we have in the things that matter? Yet if we are able to show respect and humility to others in the less significant areas, it may open doors to further, deeper conversations.

Practice humility. Feel free to disagree, but insist on disagreeing respectfully.

Field Notes

- <u>We know disrespect when we see it—or give it</u>. Respect and its manifestations are cultural, but we can almost always tell when we (or others) are disrespectful. This means that our disrespect will not go unnoticed, particularly when we are in adversarial discussions.

- <u>Respect usually plays out in speech and treatment</u>. How do I address other people? How do I label their arguments? Do I let them finish? Do I have a condescending tone of voice? Do I belittle their position? Do I dismiss them and laugh at them?

- <u>There is a time to move on.</u> No matter how respectful our disagreement is, there is a point at which continual dialogue may be unproductive. Some people bring out the worst in us. Some people refuse to listen. There is no harm in deciding that our time and energy is better spent with other people.

CHAPTER 9:
COMPLIMENT SOMEONE

I N MANY AREAS OF LIFE, competition is unhealthy. We constantly compare ourselves to others in some imaginary game: how many friends we have, how much money or respect we have, how attractive we are. An unspoken thought undergirds this mentality: *If they succeed, we lose.* We become concerned with others only as rivals. How do their efforts, successes, and failures affect *us*? There is pride here.

Humility means breaking the power of constant competition and comparison. Compliment someone.

The Biblical Connection

Paul teaches Christians to use their mouths to help and bless others. *"Let no corrupting talk come out of your mouths, but only such as is good for building up, as fits the occasion, that it may give grace to those who hear"*(Eph 4:29). Our speech should build up, not tear down. Our speech should give grace, not heartache. Paul zeroes in on the impact our words have on others. Speaking is not simply a matter of venting or self-expression; it is a gift that can leave others better than we found them.

Jesus tells us that our speech is a reflection of our hearts. *"You brood of vipers! How can you speak good, when you are evil? For out of the abundance of the heart the mouth speaks. The good person out of his good treasure brings forth good, and the evil person out of his evil treasure brings forth evil"*(Matt 12:34-35). Corrupt talk that discourages and weakens stems from a corrupt heart. Something is sick within us when we can only criticize.

Hebrews challenges us to *"consider how to stir up one another to love and good works, not neglecting to meet together, as is the habit of some, but encouraging one another, and all the more as you see the Day drawing near"*(Heb 10:24-25). Stirring up and encouraging are primarily *verbal*. *"But exhort one another every day, as long as it is called 'today,' that none of you may be hardened by the deceitfulness of sin"*(Heb 3:13). Exhorting means using positive speech to help someone continue to do something hard. It is surprising how impactful supportive words are. Even though what we say doesn't change anything about the situation, we can give courage, hope, and positivity. God wants us to say good things about our fellow-Christians because what we say has an impact on their continued service.

Why Is This Hard?

It is easy to fail to consider others and their needs. We are just a little too busy with our own to-do lists, obligations, and plans. Even when we have a break from our own things, we want to spend it relaxing or having our own leisure time. Thinking about how to talk to others in positive ways means we must break the spell of self. Complimenting others is hard because it means <u>we have to begin by actually thinking about them</u>.

One challenge of complimenting others is that <u>we carry emotional baggage into the situation</u>. Sometimes we've been hurt, so we don't *want* to speak positively. Sometimes we're jealous, so we *can't* speak positively. In such states, our speech reflects the venom in our own hearts. We want to tear down. We feel that others don't deserve our compliments. We grow to believe that complimenting others somehow detracts from ourselves. Compounding the difficulty is that we may not even see the baggage we carry; we just think someone else is that unpleasant.

Another challenge of compliments is that <u>we can easily get into ruts of negative thinking</u>. We rant about the small inconveniences and annoyances we experience. We moan about the idiosyncrasies of all the people we know. We laugh with others about people whose appearance, mannerisms, or behaviors are odd. The line between good-natured humor and sharp criticism is thin here. *It is extraordinarily rare to hear people—even Christians—who guilelessly praise others.* It always feels like the compliment is the first half of a punchline. Positivity must be learned and practiced.

How Does This Help with Humility?

Complimenting someone *sincerely*—meaning without agenda or sarcasm—will humble us.

When we compliment, <u>the spotlight is off of us</u>. Our goal is to honor others, to encourage, to give grace, and to show kindness. We are merely praising others. We are not trying to get compliments in return. This lowers us and elevates the person we praise.

Complimenting begins with *considering* others. In what areas do they excel? What do we admire about them? What is praiseworthy? What makes us happy when we are around them? How could we encourage them? This process of consideration interrupts our penchant for self-absorption and opens our eyes to the people around us.

Complimenting means that we do not view the disparity between others and ourselves as a threat. If others are praised, it doesn't detract from us. The fact that they have good attributes means nothing about me. In fact, sincere compliments have a tremendous power to break the hold of jealousy, comparison, and resentment that can build up in our hearts. Other people do things well—and that is an unqualified good. This humbles us.

Compliments mean that we will have to sift through negative characteristics to seek out the good. Everyone will have some imperfections in their character. These will draw our attention and we will be tempted toward criticism. Yet can we truly find nothing good to say about someone? Is there no room for some positivity and praise in every person? Is there no thing they do well? The exercise itself produces humility.

Practice humility. See the good in someone—and compliment them.

Field Notes

- <u>Compliment character, not appearance</u>. Appearances can be deceiving; a good-looking person can have a corrupt heart. *"Like a gold ring in a pig's snout is a beautiful woman without discretion"*(Prov 11:22). God does not evaluate people according to appearances for this reason. *" 'Do not look on his appearance or on the height of his stature, because I have rejected him. For the LORD sees not as man sees: man looks on the outward appearance, but the LORD looks on the heart'"*(1 Sam 16:7). And beauty fades with time: *"Charm is deceitful and beauty is passing, but a woman who fears the LORD, she shall be praised"*(Prov 31:30, NKJV). As we age and our looks fade, is there nothing left to compliment? The reason is that *we do not choose our appearance, but we do choose our character.* When we praise appearance, we are telling others that what matters about them is something they cannot help that won't last long. When we praise character choices, we are encouraging others to keep making those good choices and drawing closer to God.

- <u>Prepare for strange looks</u>. This is such a rare practice that the people we compliment may smell a rat. When the one we are complimenting is not present, it may seem that we are joking. On one occasion, I praised a lady for a good work I had observed. Little did I know that I was speaking to her ex-husband! Needless to say, he had a different take on her good work—and many more thoughts to share with me on her general character. Sometimes people take our compliments and feel that they have to "set the record straight" by airing their grievances.

Field Notes (continued)

- <u>Be patient</u>. As time passes and we show that this is a part of our character, the sense of strangeness will be diminished. "Good gossip" catches on.

CHAPTER 10: DO A GOOD DEED SECRETLY

A S NICE AS IT IS TO BE PRAISED, it can become a problem. We easily get addicted to being noticed and can begin to play to the crowd. We grow concerned with others knowing and acknowledging the good that we do—and in some ways we feel it validates our effort. All of this leads to an outsized sense of our own importance and impact.

Humility requires a different path—the path of secret service.

The Biblical Connection

Jesus warns his disciples about the danger of seeking to impress people. *"Beware of practicing your righteousness before other people in order to be seen by them, for then you will have no reward from your Father who is in heaven"*(Matt 6:1). He is concerned about our motives—doing things *"in order to be seen"*—not just whether others actually see us. It is inevitable that people will occasionally see us doing good, yet this shouldn't be our reason for doing it.

How do we make certain that we aren't trying to impress others rather than God? Jesus teaches us a practice that will ensure pure motives.

> *"Thus, when you give to the needy, sound no trumpet before you, as the hypocrites do in the synagogues and in the streets, that they may be praised by others. Truly, I say to you, they have received their reward. But when you give to the needy, do not let your left hand know what your right hand is doing, so that your giving may be in secret. And your Father who sees in secret will reward you"(Matt 6:2-4).*

Instead of sounding a trumpet so that others will notice, Jesus teaches us to give in secret. *"Do not let your left hand know what your right hand is doing"* means that we keep it as quiet as possible. We give so that no one knows that we have given except for God and us.

Jesus teaches this same principle about prayer: *"But when you pray, go into your room and shut the door and pray to your Father who is in secret"*(Matt 6:6). He applies it to fasting: *"But when you fast, anoint your head and wash your face, that your fasting may not be seen by others but by your Father who is in secret"*(Matt 6:17). Jesus teaches this in so many different areas that we can safely apply it to all of our good deeds.

The power of secret good deeds is that *there is no other motivation than to please God.* Only God sees and knows. If we want to impress people, why bother with secret good deeds? Of course it is possible to pray all night in our closets, then "let it slip" to someone—or to bemoan how hungry we are because we are fasting—but these are clearly against the spirit of what Jesus is saying. Do good for God and the rest will take care of itself.

Why Is This Hard?

When we are alone, the temptation is to do secret *evil* deeds. "No one will ever know" is often an excuse for some *wrong* behavior we are contemplating. We view these as opportunities to do what we really want to do, in the absence of criticism and judgment from others. Jesus is encouraging us to seize opportunities to do *evil* and use them to do *good*. In fact, he teaches us to hide our good and expose our evil—the exact opposite of our tendency.

It is nice to be complimented, noticed, and respected—especially when we are sacrificing and working hard for God. There is a positive feeling that comes from doing the right thing, which is then combined with the satisfaction of knowing that God is pleased, which is then amplified by the fact that others praise us. This cluster of pleasant sensations is hard to pass up.

Secret deeds are challenging because they require faith that God sees and will reward us. Our world tells us that if we do not make a splash, our lives and work are meaningless. We must "change the world" and "make a difference." In other words, we are trained to believe that others hold the key to our significance. Yet secret deeds trade on the promise that "*your Father who sees in secret will reward you.*" It requires a leap of faith to forgo the accolades of men to pursue the pleasure of God. There will be no parades celebrating our choices. The world will little notice. But we trust that God always sees and will reward our piety.

How Does This Help with Humility?

Secret good deeds <u>push the reset button on our motivations</u>. We help others, pray, fast, visit, minister, and give *because we love God*. We do not do it for ourselves. We do not do it to raise our status. We do not do it so that others will call attention to us and give us accolades. Serving others—where we get nothing in return—humbles us.

Secret service lowers us because we <u>deliberately avoid the applause of men</u>. It is one thing to know that we like praise; it is another thing entirely to limit situations where people even know about our praiseworthy actions. Others might have reason to honor us, but we refuse to seek it out.

Doing our works where others don't notice also <u>helps us to embrace the obscurity of quiet service</u>. What if we don't change the world? What if we don't make a difference—or at least not one we can easily measure? Does that matter if God is pleased with us? This is the opposite of sounding trumpets, praying in the streets, or disfiguring our faces. Humility does not draw attention to itself.

Practice humility. Find someone to help, pray for, send money to, show kindness to, mentor, or encourage. Find a practice like prayer, fasting, or Bible reading that is purely about your devotion to the Lord. Do it in secret.

Field Notes

- <u>The world often doesn't understand this impulse</u>. On one occasion, I attempted to give anonymously to a cause. When I went to the bank to give, the teller could not understand why I wouldn't want to be known. Perhaps billionaire donors want to keep their contributions anonymous, but everyday people hiding their good works still strikes some as strange.

- <u>Sometimes people will stumble onto our good deeds.</u> Even when we don't intend it, sometimes people will learn about or observe good things we do. Jesus is not teaching us to fear people knowing what we have done, nor is he giving us an excuse to hide things in the interest of doing wrong. So when people unexpectedly discover our good deeds, we should not feel guilty. We just can't let it affect our motives for the good deeds in the first place.

- <u>In some life-stages, it is hard to find time to do anything in secret</u>. When we had young children, there was very little space or time where they were not present. It is hard to pray in your closet when little hands poke under the door. It is hard to give to someone when little voices ask what we are doing. These are times when we need to be gracious with ourselves and do what we are able to do. In fact, it may be beneficial for our kids to see us giving, praying, fasting, and caring.

Field Notes (continued)

- <u>Don't assume others aren't doing good works just because you don't see them</u>. Occasionally people will complain to me that "no one in this church is doing anything." I find this interesting because I am often aware of people's good deeds that others are not. It is a rich blessing to stumble on others' good deeds— someone who has been visiting or praying or cooking or studying. If Jesus specifically tells us not to do our good deeds to be seen, then we shouldn't be surprised when Christians do good works that we don't see.

CHAPTER 11: LET SOMEONE ELSE DECIDE

W E ALL HAVE PREFERENCES. We want our way. We long for control over our lives and circumstances—and that impulse can lead us to demand the right to build our lives according to our liking. The trouble comes when we have to deal with others who have *their* own preferences and want *their* own way.

Humility comes when we forgo our will and let someone else decide.

The Biblical Connection

Abram and Lot (uncle and nephew) are living together in the land of Canaan. God has blessed them so that their flocks, herds, and people are so numerous that "*the land could not support both of them dwelling together*"(Gen 13:6). So Abram makes a suggestion:

> "*Then Abram said to Lot, 'Let there be no strife between you and me, and between your herdsmen and my herdsmen, for we are kinsmen. Is not the whole land before you? Separate yourself from me. If you take the left hand, then I will go to the right, or if you take the*

right hand, then I will go to the left.' And Lot lifted up his eyes and saw that the Jordan Valley was well watered everywhere like the garden of the LORD...So Lot chose for himself all the Jordan Valley, and Lot journeyed east. Thus they separated from each other. Abram settled in the land of Canaan, while Lot settled among the cities of the valley and moved his tent as far as Sodom"(Gen 13:8–12).

Abram has every right—as the older man, the uncle, and probably the wealthier—to make this decision himself. He can tell Lot what to do. Instead, he yields to Lot. Abram does not insist on the best land or throw his weight around or lecture Lot about respecting his elders. He lets Lot decide.

In giving Lot the choice, Abram surrenders himself to Lot. If Lot chooses a different path, then perhaps it is Abram who winds up in Sodom. Yet he is willing to lower himself before his nephew. There is humility here.

The New Testament teaches the importance of being willing to submit to others. We do not always get our way. We are to *"be subject to the governing authorities"*(Rom 13:1). In a local church, we are told to *"obey your leaders and submit to them, for they are keeping watch over your souls"*(Heb 13:17). Wives are to *"submit to your own husbands, as to the Lord"*(Eph 5:22). Servants are to *"be subject to your masters with all respect"*(1 Pet 2:18). And Christians of all sorts, classes, and genders are to live *"submitting to one another out of reverence for Christ"*(Eph 5:21). Letting someone else decide is common practice for disciples of Jesus.

In discussing the nature of love to the Corinthians (who are struggling to practice it), Paul writes that love *"does not insist on its own way"*(1 Cor 13:5). Love is not demanding and forceful; it leaves room for others to make decisions—even if they are not our favorite.

Why Is This Hard?

Letting others decide is hard because <u>we want what we want</u>! We want to decide. Otherwise we are at the mercy of others who might not make the best choices. That stretches from simple decisions (where we'll eat for dinner) to major ones (where we'll move). When we make poor decisions, at least we have no one to blame but ourselves. But putting ourselves in the hands of others whose judgment we can't always trust is extremely challenging.

We have all have had negative experiences that stemmed from others' poor choices, especially in childhood. Often becoming an adult means that we get the freedom to decide—and we grow determined to never go through those kinds of experiences again. Letting others decide <u>opens us up to the pain, discomfort, and frustration of outcomes we cannot control</u>.

Sometimes our desire to control things is about a hunger for power. In chapter 7, we learned about Diotrephes *"who likes to put himself first"*(3 John 9) and so resists the apostles and expels people from the church. Local churches break down when we refuse to submit ourselves to others and their decisions. Letting others decide places us below others—which means that it <u>forces us to surrender power</u>.

This is also a unique challenge for Americans. Our culture stresses individual rights. We believe we should always be able to do what we want, even if it is self-destructive. So ceding those rights over to others seems almost un-American.

How Does This Help with Humility?

Letting others decide means that we submit ourselves to them. We forfeit the opportunity to be in charge. We leave off insisting on our own rights. We are comfortable with things not being ideal. Like Abram, we may get the short end of whatever decision is made—yet we willingly sign up for it. As noted above, there are some situations in which we *must* submit and obey. We cannot really think that by obeying traffic laws we are letting someone else decide. We practice humility by *choosing* to let others decide when we could just as easily insist on our own way. We lower ourselves.

One of our most dangerous illusions is the notion that we are masters of our own destinies. Our clothes, homes, and cars are statements of what we like and want. Our phones offer us a completely customizable experience. Websites tell us which music and movies they think we will like. We eat where we like—or have someone bring it to us. We live like modern royalty. This leads inexorably to pride. We become frustrated when we cannot have our way in any situation. We have no patience for inconvenience. We begin to want other people to fall in line with our wishes. Letting other people decide banishes the myth that our lives are in our control. It reminds us that other people view the world differently—and that this can benefit us. It exposes us to thought processes and priorities that are outside ourselves. When we deliberately place ourselves in others' hands, we are strongly reminded that we are not masters of our own destinies.

Practice humility. Let someone else decide where you eat—
where you go—what you talk about—who gets invited. Let others
decide how to do something. Let them choose methods that annoy
or frustrate you. Put yourself in their hands. Let co-workers have
the say. Do things their way. Let someone else decide.

Field Notes

- <u>There is a time to assert ourselves</u>. I am not advocating
  for abusive relationships. There are people in our lives
  who want to control us and would love for us to give
  them the reins. Sometimes they will try to pressure us
  into doing things that are evil—or not good for us—or
  that violate our boundaries. It is important to say
  "enough" to toxic situations. Yet this does not change
  the fact that in the majority of our interactions with
  others we still want what we want—and letting go of
  those decisions will help us humble ourselves.

CHAPTER 12: REFUSE TO COMPLAIN

WHINING IS A NATIONAL PASTIME. It dominates our conversations, despite the fact that America is extraordinarily prosperous. Social media is abuzz with it; we post complaints and then complain about the complaints of others. We grumble about political and economic problems, about sports and hobbies, about traffic and weather.

Humility demands a different course. Refuse to complain.

The Biblical Connection

Paul not only encourages Christians to quit complaining, but also notes that it will make us different from the world. *"Do all things without grumbling or disputing, that you may be blameless and innocent, children of God without blemish in the midst of a crooked and twisted generation, among whom you shine as lights in the world"* (Phil 2:14-15). Paul (who incidentally is writing from a prison cell) asserts that we can live without grumbling or disputing. We can't avoid negative circumstances, but complaining about them is a choice we don't have to make. When we stop complaining and arguing, we *"shine as lights in the world.*" Our talk will be so markedly different from the world that we will be lights shining in a dark place. The absence of complaining will help our influence.

Paul also calls to mind the Israelites who, after the exodus, were overcome with complaining in wandering through the desert: "*nor grumble, as some of them did and were destroyed by the Destroyer*"(1 Cor 10:10). They complain when they find no water. They complain when they don't like the food choices, particularly when there is not enough meat. They complain when things take too long. They complain about their leaders. Their complaining frustrates and angers God, often leading to their deaths. Their example reminds us that complaining feeds on itself and becomes a mentality. We get so accustomed to complaining that we are constantly on the lookout for the next problem.

The Bible also warns us that there are some situations in which we are more likely to complain than others. "*Show hospitality to one another without grumbling*"(1 Pet 4:9). Hospitality involves welcoming and providing for someone, especially strangers. The danger in hospitality is that it can be so taxing and exhausting that we resent it. We welcome others, but we complain about it. Peter warns that this attitude tends to invalidate whatever service we do. What good is our gift if we complain about giving it?

Why Is This Hard?

Sometimes life is hard and unpleasant. It is only natural for us to give voice to that. When we are frustrated by a person or situation, we tend to say something. The problem is that it easily becomes a habit that is extremely difficult to break. We become so immersed in our complaints that <u>we do not even notice what we are doing</u>.

Our culture also encourages and rewards complaining. We give more attention to a person with a problem or irritation than one who tells us everything is fine. So there is a temptation to fabricate or overstate problems to get attention from others. Refusing to complain might mean learning an entirely new way to talk and relate to others.

It is also possible to <u>confuse complaining with openness</u>. Scripture teaches us to share our life-struggles and bear one another's burdens (Gal 6:1-2). Yet sometimes we are not sharing, but venting and whining. In the interest of being "real" or "authentic" or "open" we give voice to every slight annoyance or mild discomfort. Then we complain (!) that those who don't share such complaints aren't being "real"! There are times when life becomes overwhelming and we are deeply troubled, but we don't have to complain just to have something to talk about. It can be hard to tell the difference.

How Does This Help with Humility?

The discipline of not complaining teaches us that <u>we don't have to have an ideal life to be happy</u>. When we complain, we imply that we *deserve* to have every part of our life be free of inconvenience or annoyance. This is a pride issue. We can find other things to discuss, other blessings to appreciate, and other thoughts to consider. Negativity doesn't have to rule. Things don't have to be perfect for us to have joy and be at peace.

Refusing to complain gives fuel to some humbling—and liberating—thoughts. We don't have to give voice to every unpleasantness. There is virtue to suffering small indignities in silence. We can simply acknowledge and praise God for the good in our lives and the small joys in life. We know that we don't deserve them.

Refusing to complain redeems our relationships. God's goal for relationships is not that we can have someone sit still while we whine at them. Having others lament with us, "Oh, that's terrible!" is not the same as a meaningful connection. While there is a place for honestly discussing serious problems, we can easily cross the line into the realm of serial complaining. When we refuse to complain, we free up our relationships to be focused on what we love, how God has blessed us, and what we are excited about. It helps us with humility because it reminds us that others are not there simply to take our complaining.

Similarly, refusing to complain will deepen our relationship with God. We must remember that God's purpose is not merely to create a rose-strewn path for us. This is the height of pride. In fact, Scripture teaches us that God often has deeper plans at play than our comfort (see James 1:2-4). It may be that God's goal is to lead us through the difficulty we currently face so that we develop stronger, more mature character. How sad if we fight God's purposes and adamantly resist his leading because it involves adversity! Submitting to God's will without complaining humbles us.

Practice humility. Take some time—I recommend to start with an hour or so—and refuse to complain. Discover other topics that worthy of your time and attention—things that are true, honorable, just, pure, lovely, commendable, excellent, and praiseworthy (Phil 4:8). Enjoy conversation that leaves everyone feeling more positive. Monitor your speech so that nothing that comes out of your mouth could be construed as complaining. You may find that this exercise is harder than you expect.

Practice humility. Refuse to complain.

Field Notes

- <u>Listen for others' complaining—but don't complain about it!</u> Once I started monitoring my own speech for complaining, I heard it everywhere! So many conversations default to what we're unhappy about in our health, kids, jobs, country, or sports team. When you hear it, note the scope of the problem—but don't complain!

- <u>Beware mindless complaining.</u> In my efforts to limit my own complaining, I found that a lot of my complaining was about things that I wasn't really very upset about. One morning I complained about so many bodily ailments that my wife couldn't keep track of them all. I regularly would start my day with "I'm tired" or "I'm hungry" or "I'm dreading this or that." I started to hear it in my kids as well. Deeply upsetting problems happen, but they are usually not a daily occurrence. Watch out for the negative tone of mindless complaining.

Field Notes (continued)

- <u>We still have to relate negative information</u>. Not everything is pleasant. We may still need to talk about it. What is the difference between saying something necessary that is negative and complaining? I find it helpful to ask myself the question, "What is my goal in saying this?". If there is a legitimate need, then I proceed. If I am merely frustrated, I (usually!) hold back.

- <u>Prepare to be happier</u>. Happiness is not the same as humility, but I must add how surprising it was to find myself significantly happier when I cut back on complaining. Other people enjoyed me more. My conversations were better. My mood lightened. I was more grateful. It may be that you discover—as I did—that you were the source of a lot of your own unhappiness.

CHAPTER 13: BE NICE TO SOMEONE UNDESERVING

S OME PEOPLE DON'T DESERVE KINDNESS. Maybe we have a history with them. Or it could be that their personality is unpleasant. Some people are mean-spirited and we tend to operate on a "I'll treat you the way you treat me" basis with them.

Yet this can have consequences. We easily grow condescending toward such people. Maybe we don't always act as we should, but we are *certainly* not like *them*! Thus the unpleasant traits of others lead to our pride.

To break this spell, be nice to someone undeserving.

The Biblical Connection

Saul is Israel's first king, yet his appointment is not without controversy. While most of the nation celebrates their new leader, *"some worthless fellows said, 'How can this man save us?' And they despised him and brought him no present. But he held his peace"*(1 Sam

10:27). When Saul leads the armies of Israel to victory over the Ammonites, some of the people remember these naysayers. "*Then the people said to Samuel, 'Who is it that said, "Shall Saul reign over us?" Bring the men, that we may put them to death.' But Saul said, 'Not a man shall be put to death this day, for today the LORD has worked salvation in Israel'*"(1 Sam 11:12-13). Now that Saul has a stronger hand, some suggest that he kill those men—both as an act of justice and a consolidation of power. But Saul refuses. He has mercy. Saul shows great humility here—he is "*little in (his) own eyes*"(1 Sam 15:17)—because he is kind to the undeserving.

King David has a similar experience. When his son Absalom takes his throne by a coup, David and his entourage flee Jerusalem. Shimei—a relative of Saul—curses David, kicking him when he is down (2 Sam 16:5-8). It is not long before Absalom is defeated and David returns to Jerusalem. Who is groveling before him? It's Shimei, begging for mercy! Just like Saul, David pardons: "*Shall anyone be put to death in Israel this day? For do I not know that I am this day king over Israel?*"(2 Sam 19:22). David shows humility by giving mercy.

When Jesus challenges his disciples to love others, he highlights the fact that love includes the undeserving. "*But I say to you who hear, Love your enemies, do good to those who hate you, bless those who curse you, pray for those who abuse you. To one who strikes you on the cheek, offer the other also, and from one who takes away your cloak do not withhold your tunic either*"(Luke 6:27-29). This kind of love is grace—a gift that their behavior does not warrant. Jesus is emphasizing that this kind of grace makes us like God, who does not wait for people to be worthy before he blesses them (Luke 6:35).

And just in case we miss it, Jesus repeats and stresses that this is the opposite of what we tend to do. *"If you love those who love you, what benefit is that to you? For even sinners love those who love them. And if you do good to those who do good to you, what benefit is that to you? For even sinners do the same. And if you lend to those from whom you expect to receive, what credit is that to you? Even sinners lend to sinners, to get back the same amount"*(Luke 6:32–34). Three times Jesus reiterates our obligation to actively seek to be kind to undeserving people. If we miss the challenge in this, we need to read his words again.

Why Is This Hard?

The difficulty here is simple: it's hard to be nice to undeserving people because <u>they don't deserve it</u>. We tend to be nice to those who are nice to us. We have warm feelings toward nice people because they have made us feel good. There is also a principle of reciprocity at play: our kindness is a down payment on future kindness from them. Undeserving people offer no such guarantees; in fact, we can almost be certain of the opposite.

When others are hateful, mean-spirited, offensive, or hurtful, <u>we sometimes feel afraid that kindness will erase or justify how they have acted</u>. We feel that such a situation demands confrontation and resistance, not kindness. Otherwise, we have let them "get away with it."

Tied closely to that is the fear that if we are kind to them, <u>they will take advantage of our kindness</u>. It can feel like we are teaching them to treat us harshly without consequence. If I turn my other cheek when you hit me, your first wrong is forgotten and a second wrong is more likely. What good is that?

There are some things to consider here. Jesus is not proposing that we have no recourse in abusive relationships. Nor is he arguing that there is never a place for confrontation (see Matt 18:15, for example). *What the Bible is teaching us is that there is a blessing in giving mercy when others don't deserve it.* We will naturally want our vengeance, but God has planned a different path for us.

How Does This Help with Humility?

<u>Insistence on vengeance stems from pride</u>. Every minor offense done to me must be avenged (and avenged by *me*). When others hurt or upset me, they should suffer! Meanwhile the harm and hurt I have caused others should be forgiven and forgotten. It's really not that big a deal! You just need to get over it! When this attitude is full-grown, we don't even notice the double standard.

But kindness to the undeserving <u>takes a different approach</u>: we're not really that important. We can let it go. Wrongs done to us are not that bad. It could be worse. We've done wrong ourselves. Our pain is real—and must be dealt with and worked through—but we can still put it aside and show mercy. We can trust God to avenge what needs avenging.

When we show kindness, we lower ourselves and put others above us. But lowering ourselves before someone who has *done us wrong* requires a more intense humility. It makes us like Jesus.

Practice humility. Single out someone who does not deserve your kindness, interest, or goodwill. Speak kindly to them. Say a

positive word about them to others. Look for the good in them.
Show interest. Give a gift. Treat them like a friend.

It could be that such a course unlocks a flood of goodwill from
them. It could be that a chain of kindness and grace could begin
with you. Or it could be that they ignore or deride you. Either way,
you will have practiced humility.

Practice humility. Be nice to someone undeserving.

Field Notes

- <u>Stifle your initial response</u>. When others are undeserving of our kindness—whether because they have actively hurt us or merely because of some unpleasant trait—they prompt a reaction. They anger us. Sometimes we are just deeply hurt. Occasionally we might even feel disgust at them. I have found that while these emotions help me to know that I am upset, they are not helpful in treating others well. To be nice to someone undeserving, we will have to consciously overrule these emotions and not allow them to determine our tone in talking to them.

- <u>It helps to not dwell on why they are undeserving</u>. I have sometimes found myself fixating on what someone has done to me, nursing my wound and the bitterness it has caused in me. It has been liberating for me to find other things to focus on—seeking out the good in them, remembering when I have done ugly things to others, and reminding myself that every person is made in the image of God. But if we only focus on others' worst traits and deeds, it should not surprise us when we struggle to be kind to them.

CHAPTER 14: APPLY THE BIBLE TO YOUR FAULTS

I T IS DEEPLY IRONIC THAT the most religious people can have the worst pride problems. Their stories saturate the Bible—from Solomon (who saw Jehovah twice yet turned away from him) to Eli's sons (who abused their position as priests to get all the food and women they wanted). History is littered with corrupt religious figures, but the problem is not merely hypocrisy. Somewhere along the way, their religion no longer stems the tide of their pride.

The tragedy is that in their pursuit of God, they fall headlong into the sin that is most abhorrent to him.

Don't be like them. Apply the Bible to your faults.

The Biblical Connection

The Bible describes the proper attitude in which to read the Bible. In the Old Testament, God speaks of one who is *"humble and contrite in spirit and trembles at my word"*(Isa 66:2). Ezra speaks of those who *"trembled at the words of the God of Israel"*(Ezra 9:4) and who *"tremble at the commandment of our God"*(Ezra 10:3). Trembling at the words of God indicates a posture of humility. If we truly believe that God is God, his words are not to be treated lightly—particularly when we have not kept them.

James gives the New Testament counterpart to this image: *"Therefore put away all filthiness and rampant wickedness and receive with meekness the implanted word, which is able to save your souls"* (James 1:21). *"Meekness"* here is a synonym for humility. God wants us to humble ourselves beneath his words, submitting ourselves to him.

Yet the Bible also warns that there is a danger that we will receive God's word *without* meekness or trembling. It is easy to see others in the word of God and not see ourselves. After King David—a very religious person—has an affair with Bathsheba, has her husband killed, and marries her himself, God sends the prophet Nathan to confront him. Nathan tells him a story about a rich man who, instead of providing a meal from his own flocks and herds, steals a poor man's only lamb. David thinks that this is merely a case of egregious theft—not seeing himself in the story. He pronounces that the man will surely die and restore four times as many lambs (presumably before dying).

In some of the most chilling words in Scripture, Nathan says to David, *"You are the man!"* (2 Sam 12:7). Nathan outlines all that David has done, driving the lesson home with full force. He pronounces God's verdict and judgment. *"David said to Nathan, 'I have sinned against the LORD'"* (2 Sam 12:13). Humility has been restored.

David's example shows us that <u>we must beware hearing words from God and thinking they are not meant for us</u>. Paul tells

Timothy that *"all Scripture is breathed out by God and profitable for teaching, for reproof, for correction, and for training in righteousness, that the man of God may be complete, equipped for every good work"*(2 Tim 3:16-17). God intends his word to teach and train us to become the people he wants us to be. This only happens if we take his word and actively apply it to the areas of our lives that need *"reproof"* and *"correction"* and *"training."*

Paul also makes personal and direct application of the Israelites in the desert to Gentile converts thousands of years later. *"Now these things took place as examples for us, that we might not desire evil as they did...Now these things happened to them as an example, but they were written down for our instruction, on whom the end of the ages has come"*(1 Cor 10:6, 11). He stresses that each part of their experience—and each flaw they exhibited—is a warning to us. They are temptations that are *"common to man"*(1 Cor 10:13). So we—though removed in time and space—must learn to *"let anyone who thinks that he stands take heed lest he fall"*(1 Cor 10:12). This is the way the Bible is to be used.

Jesus informs many of the Jews of his day that the reason they reject him is their failure to truly understand Scripture. *"For if you believed Moses, you would believe me; for he wrote of me. But if you do not believe his writings, how will you believe my words?"*(John 5:46-47). He directly challenges the Pharisees: *"Go and learn what this means, 'I desire mercy, and not sacrifice.' For I came not to call the righteous, but sinners"*(Matt 9:13). Their responses to him— especially their rejection of his compassion—shows that they have not applied this passage to their own thinking. *They know the Bible, but their failure to apply it to themselves leads them to reject Jesus.*

Many Christian thinkers, steeped in biblical thinking, press us to do more than simply read the Bible. Bernard of Clairvaux warns that "the interpreter must see himself in that which is said."[6] In a discourse on Job, Gregory the Great muses that "we understand the words of God more truly when we 'search out [ourselves] in them.'"[7] Origen tells us that it is not enough to say that Christ was crucified: "One must say, with St Paul, 'I am crucified with Christ'(Gal 2:20). Likewise it is not enough to say 'Christ is raised'; one who knows Christ says, 'We shall also live with him'(Rom 6:8)."[8] We must see ourselves—warts and all—in Scripture.

Why Is This Hard?

Applying the Bible to ourselves—especially the parts that are unflattering—is hard because <u>it is much easier to focus on others and their faults</u>. Jesus warns us of this tendency: *"Why do you see the speck that is in your brother's eye, but do not notice the log that is in your own eye?"*(Matt 7:3). We prefer to think about others and their flaws because correcting our own is a lot of unpleasant work. So the Bible becomes a way to hear someone correct the people and characteristics we don't like. We relish sermons where the preacher "tells off" groups or attributes we find distasteful. We look around to see if others are listening—the people whom we think "need to hear this." We lament the awful state of our society, the opposing political party, and kids these days. We shake our heads and cluck our tongues. All this condescension is much easier than doing the hard work of changing *ourselves* in obedience to God's word.

---

[6] Cited in Wilken, p. 77.

[7] Cited in Wilken, p. 78.

[8] Cited in Kovacs, p. xvii.

This is hard because <u>we are often in denial about ourselves</u>. We don't see ourselves clearly and we often judge ourselves by a different (read: more lenient) standard than we do others. Applying the Bible to our faults means we must admit we have faults—and that's hard.

<u>Bible interpretation is also sometimes difficult</u>, leaving us some room to skirt by its application. I have noticed this tendency about Jesus' teaching on lust (Matt 5:27-30). All manner of justifications are given that gut his words of their meaning ("I'm just admiring her beauty" or "God made men to be visually attracted"). But the same trend is found in any topic that contains subjectivity: what exactly constitutes gossip or jealousy, what clothes Christians should wear, or what curse words cross the line. *When there is any question of interpretation, we naturally tend to apply the Bible in the way that justifies what we are already comfortable doing.* This makes sincere, humbling application hard.

Sometimes we <u>confuse *identifying* our faults with *changing* them</u>. There is a huge difference between admitting some character flaw ("I've got a temper!") and actually working to change it. While the Bible is key to self-discovery and self-examination, this is not the endpoint of Bible study. Once we know ourselves and our tendencies, the real work begins. What are we going to do about it?

Most of all, applying Scripture to our faults challenges us because <u>we don't like to think of ourselves in need of correction</u>. We either want to pretend our faults don't exist (denial) or that we can never change them (fatalism). We must admit we are not perfect—and that growing and changing in obedience to God is our responsibility.

How Does This Help with Humility?

When David is confronted, he is immediately humbled. "*I have sinned.*" There can be no pride in these words. <u>Acknowledging our flaws and weakness means that we are not trying to save face</u>. There is no press conference to spin this in the best way. We have no excuses. Layers of pride fall away as we kneel before the truth of what we have done and beg God's forgiveness.

This posture means that <u>we come to Scripture with a new perspective: I may be wrong</u>. God has something to say to *me*. I am not right because I am me. I have work to do. We begin to connect to the stories of the Bible in a much deeper way. We relate to these people and their flaws because we have flaws as well. We see the great value in God's mercy because we see how deeply we need it. We want God to work in us because we see that we cannot be trusted to successfully lead ourselves.

Applying God's word this way also <u>helps us to not be as critical and condescending toward others</u>. Jesus continues with the speck and beam illustration: "*You hypocrite, first take the log out of your own eye, and then you will see clearly to take the speck out of your brother's eye*"(Matt 7:5). When we are applying Scripture to ourselves first, our approach to others changes. We are merely helping them clean up what we have already been working on in ourselves. We all have our specks and beams. There is no room for superiority.

This is where the rubber meets the road of our faith. Will we allow God to speak to us and submit to his will in every area of our lives? Will we humble ourselves before him?

Practice humility. In reading and studying Scripture, ask: What are my faults? What does God think? How can I change? How does this challenge me? What am I afraid of?

Practice humility. Apply the Bible to your faults.

Field Notes

- <u>Start with an awareness of your faults</u>. Each of us has a unique personality. We think and act in ways that are deeply ingrained. There is good and bad in all of us. It is important that we be aware of the particular ways in which we personally battle with sin. Where have we fallen before? What Bible words describe our tendencies and weaknesses? What have others noticed about us that is unpleasant or evil? Where do we have work to do? With this awareness, we can find things in each part of the Bible that speak directly to us.

- <u>Try to humanize the stories.</u> We tend to make Bible stories into fables. David seems superhuman before Goliath. Abraham seems to have a nearly robotic faith in sacrificing Isaac. It helps me to view these people as people (see James 5:17). They also gravitate toward pride. They get tired. They sometimes choose bad friends. Yet they also show the transformative power and courage of faith. We are challenged when we see that they are like us, yet still serve God faithfully.

CHAPTER 15: QUESTION YOUR ANGER

L IKE PAIN, ANGER IS A SENSATION that tells us that something is wrong. Something we care about has been threatened or insulted. The problem is that not everything we get angry about (and not everything we do while angry) is justified.

Don't assume your anger is appropriate. Question your anger.

The Biblical Connection

Jonah's story is about more than a big fish. God commissions him to preach a message of repentance to the people of Nineveh, the capital of Assyria. Jonah is reluctant. These people are infamous for their cruelty. Jonah feels that they are unworthy of God's warning or his mercy. He wants to see them punished, not saved. So when they repent and God spares them, Jonah gets mad.

> *"But it displeased Jonah exceedingly, and he became angry. So he prayed to the LORD, and said, 'Ah, LORD, was*

not this what I said when I was still in my country?
Therefore I fled previously to Tarshish; for I know that
You are a gracious and merciful God, slow to anger and
abundant in lovingkindness, One who relents from
doing harm. Therefore now, O Lord*, please take my life*
from me, for it is better for me to die than to live!' Then
the Lord *said, 'Is it right for you to be angry?'"*(Jonah
4:1-4, NKJV)

God asks Jonah, *"Is it right for you to be angry?"* because not all
anger is justified. Jonah's anger shows that his heart is not in the
right place. God wants him to question his anger.

After this, as he sits in the desert watching the city, God causes a
plant to grow, giving him shade. When the plant dies, Jonah is
again angry.

"Then he wished death for himself, and said, 'It is better
for me to die than to live.' Then God said to Jonah, 'Is it
right for you to be angry about the plant?' And he said,
'It is right for me to be angry, even to death!'(Jonah
4:8-9, NKJV)

Jonah sounds like a petulant child. His anger is not right.

Paul teaches Jesus' disciples to *"be angry and do not sin; do not let*
the sun go down on your anger, and give no opportunity to the devil"(Eph
4:26-27). *"Be angry and do not sin"* means that anger is not wrong
in itself, yet it also strongly implies that anger can lead us to sin.
Anger is a state in which sin is more likely. We are less in control
of our words and actions. This is why Scripture abounds with
warnings against being easily or regularly angered (James 1:19-21,

Prov 14:29, 19:11, 16:32, 15:18, 29:22, 14:17). We need the humility to ask ourselves whether our anger is appropriate.

The Bible does tell us about "righteous anger"—the state in which we are provoked by a threat or insult to God. Jesus is angered by the hardness of his contemporaries' hearts (Mark 3:5) and certainly appears to have some anger when he drives the sellers and moneychangers out of the temple (John 2:13-17). Moses is angry with Pharaoh's hard heart and with the people's golden calf. But the most important thing we can say about "righteous anger" is that *it is not personal.* It's not about our own personal frustrations, concerns, or honor. In these examples, righteous anger springs from egregious evil and dishonoring of *God.* We must admit that the vast majority of the times we get angry, it is about us. So claiming that our anger is righteous doesn't exempt us from the vital process of questioning our anger.

Why Is This Hard?

Questioning our anger is hard because <u>we don't want to stop ourselves when we get angry</u>. We *feel* right, so that even when others question us, we rarely consider it. Like Jonah, we blow right through questions and warnings. *"It is right for me to be angry, even to death!"* We don't even realize how silly we sound. We are not interested in careful evaluation of our emotions and their appropriateness. We are usually more concerned about venting our anger.

We get angry when something we care about is threatened, yet it is extremely hard when agitated to honestly consider whether we *should* care about it (or whether it *is* threatened). <u>The intensity of</u>

our emotions clouds our judgment. Productive conversation is remarkably difficult, much less honest self-examination.

Anger also often becomes a habit. If we grew up in a family with lots of displays of anger, we get used to expressing ourselves with little thought of whether we should. "We all have a temper." "I just tell it like it is." "You know how I am." "If you don't want me to react that way, you shouldn't say things like that to me." By linking our behavior to some personality trait, we habitually exempt ourselves from scrutiny.

How Does This Help with Humility?

Questioning our anger will help us gain distance from our feelings and the assumption that we are right. We submit our feelings to the will of God. We consider the possibility that we are wrong, even though we are mad. We lower ourselves.

Often our anger is about reactions to people. Questioning our anger will give us clarity about why we are responding the way that we are. We have probably all had the experience of feeling angry yet being unable to explain precisely why. Questioning helps us see that very often our anger stems from pride, jealousy, and selfishness.

We tend to get angry about things that don't even matter that much: small slights, moments when we are embarrassed, times we feel criticized, decisions we don't like. Why do these become huge disagreements? Once our anger is activated, we become concerned with having our feelings validated. We want to win the argument. We are right and they are wrong! We will not yield. We grow proud and demanding. We insist on our way. Sometimes we will go so far as to sacrifice the relationship so that we do not have to compromise our position! There is tremendous pride here, yet we are often too angry to perceive it. Questioning our anger will <u>help us evaluate what is truly important to us—and whether this argument or confrontation is helping us achieve our goals</u>.

Practice humility. Ask yourself:
- Is it right for me to be angry?
- Why am I so mad about this?
- What is it about this that bothers me?
- Is this a righteous emotion?
- Is this really that big a deal?
- Am I willing to hurt this relationship to be proven right?
- Do I just have my feelings hurt?
- Is this causing me to act inappropriately, invalidating my point?

Practice humility. Question your anger.

Field Notes

- <u>Back up and you'll limit your apologies</u>. This chapter deeply challenged me. For several weeks, I had a number of verbal clashes with my wife. (After the fact I realized that I had instigated them all). They followed a predictable pattern: I suffered some perceived slight, spoke out of my anger, and refused to back down. In each case, I felt remarkably, undeniably *right*. Yet as more time passed and the intensity died down, I started to realize that I was probably wrong. That sense grew until I came back to my wife and apologized for my poor behavior. The lesson I learned here is that *even if I feel I'm right, there's a good chance I am wrong.* If I stop myself sooner, I have fewer apologies to make and far less relational damage to undo.

- <u>Don't break the dam</u>. This passage was helpful to me: "*Starting a quarrel is like breaching a dam; so drop the matter before a dispute breaks out*"(Prov 17:14, NIV). It pictures our relationships as dams; when we start an argument, we make a breach. We know what comes next: another leak springs somewhere else. Soon larger and larger pieces of the dam start to break loose. Before long the whole structure collapses. Solomon's advice is to "*drop the matter before a dispute breaks out*." The vast majority of the issues that cause conflict in our relationships just don't matter. Can't we drop it? Don't break the dam over something silly.

CHAPTER 16: SAY THANK YOU

S OMETIMES SIMPLE ACTS ARE HUGE perspective-changers. Americans battle the cultural identity of being a "self-made" people. Many truly believe that economic success and social advancement are merely about our own work ethic. When we succeed, we get all the credit. We conveniently forget all the gifts, kindnesses, and encouragement others give us. We grow arrogant and self-absorbed.

Humility comes when we learn to say "thank you."

The Biblical Connection

Christians are a thankful people. Notice how many times Paul instructs us to give thanks:

> "And let the peace of Christ rule in your hearts, to which indeed you were called in one body. And <u>be thankful</u>. Let the word of Christ dwell in you richly, teaching and admonishing one another in all wisdom, singing psalms and hymns and spiritual songs, with <u>thankfulness</u> in

your hearts to God. And whatever you do, in word or deed, do everything in the name of the Lord Jesus, giving thanks to God the Father through him"(Col 3:15-17, emphasis mine).

We are thankful when we see the unity we have with other believers. We are thankful when Christ's word dwells in us, overflowing into our songs. And we are thankful as we do our work that God has blessed us so richly in Christ. This is a habit characteristic of Christians. We are a people *"abounding in thanksgiving"*(Col 2:7).

Scripture teaches us not only to be thankful to God, but thankful to others (and for others). *"First of all, then, I urge that supplications, prayers, intercessions, and thanksgivings be made for all people"*(1 Tim 2:1). Paul lists several types of prayers with different tones and purposes, but he specifies that we can be thankful to God for other people. Thanking God for other people sounds odd to our ears, but it is common in Paul's epistles: *"I give thanks to my God always for you"*(1 Cor 1:4), *"I do not cease to give thanks for you, remembering you in my prayers"*(Eph 1:16), *"we always thank God, the Father of our Lord Jesus Christ, when we pray for you"*(Col 1:3). The spirit of gratitude is not limited to God, but extends to all the good we see others do for us that makes us glad that they are around.

There is a spiritual danger to ingratitude. When Paul describes the moral devolution of the Gentiles, he begins with their lack of gratitude: *"For although they knew God, they did not honor him as God or give thanks to him, but they became futile in their thinking, and their foolish hearts were darkened"*(Rom 1:21). Things get worse from there and degenerate into a laundry list of scandalous sins. It all begins with not giving thanks. In fact, Paul shows us here that gratitude keeps our thinking fresh and healthy. Without it our thoughts become *"futile"* and *"darkened."* There is something deeply sick about the spirit that accepts good from God and others without voicing appreciation. It is a spiritual warning sign.

So a healthy spirit is summed up with three inner disciplines: *"Rejoice always, pray without ceasing, give thanks in all circumstances; for this is the will of God in Christ Jesus for you"*(1 Thess 5:16-18). Gratitude *"in all circumstances"* means that it is always possible— *always possible*—to give thanks. There is always good floating into our lives. There are always positives to see in the people around us. There is always joy in God's blessings. The struggle is being willing to see it—and to say thanks.

Why Is This Hard?

Gratitude is hard because <u>it is a habit</u>. Habits are hard to form and maintain. Overhauling the habit of ingratitude will require work and energy that we may not feel like devoting to it. If it feels unnatural or awkward, it is easier to fall back on old habits.

"Thank you" is overused in our culture. We say "thank you for your time" and "thank you for not smoking" and "thanks, everybody." At some point the words lose their meaning. Saying "thank you" <u>often feels fake or insincere</u>.

<u>We don't always remember</u> to say thank you. When Jesus heals ten lepers, only one of them comes back to thank him and praise God (Luke 17:11-19). We get that. When we receive awesome blessings, we are so excited (or relieved) that we sometimes just forget.

Some things are expected and don't deserve a thank you. We don't thank our boss for our paycheck. We don't thank the electric company for providing our service. We don't thank our friends for being nice. The danger is that <u>we begin to think that gratitude doesn't have a place in everyday life</u>.

Gratitude is hard because <u>we get used to things</u>. We keep receiving, day after day, gifts from God. We get our daily bread every day. The sun rises each day. We continue to live. Even special new blessings that we waited and prayed for—like a spouse, or children, or a home, or a job—become harder to be thankful for as their novelty wears off.

But most of all, gratitude is hard because <u>we battle selfishness</u>. So we either don't notice the gift or feel we deserve it—or both.

How Does this Help with Humility?

Saying thank you teaches us that <u>we are not self-made</u>. It acknowledges that all the opportunities we have, people we know, health we enjoy, and skills we possess are gifts we do not deserve. Our very lives are a gift from our maker. Is there anything that we can honestly say is purely our own doing? Has God not had a part? Have others not helped and blessed us? Boasting and pride come from assuming we have no one to thank. Humility comes when we say thank you.

Gratitude means that <u>we are accepting kindness from others</u>. This puts us in a lower position. *They* are the benefactor bestowing grace on *us*. We show our need and humble ourselves.

Saying thank you <u>takes the focus off of ourselves and puts it on someone else</u>. We highlight their acts of goodness and charity. We are no longer speaking about how great we are, how much we deserve such treatment, or what we are going to do with our blessing. We talk about their kindness and God's goodness.

Thankfulness also helps us to see that <u>we too have something to give</u>. Pride carries with it the belief that we are merely here to receive from others. While acknowledging the kindness of God and others *should* encourage us to do our own kindness, it also helps us see that by saying thank you, we are giving something back. We allow others to hear that their goodness found its target; they have helped us. We give them the satisfaction of knowing that they are appreciated. And so our ego goes further into the background.

Practice humility. Look at the good in your life, regardless of the situation. See the way others have done good to you. Develop a habit of noticing when others go out of their way to bless you.

Practice humility. Say thank you.

Field Notes

- <u>Explain *why* you are thankful</u>. This habit helps me battle insincerity in my gratitude. Usually, I find that I am thankful for people thinking of me specifically or for doing something unusually kind. I try to express this either in word or in writing. But this is also a helpful habit in prayer because we are explaining to God why his blessings mean so much to us.

- <u>Say little prayers</u>. Somewhere along the way we decided that prayers have to be long and formal before they count. There is value in little prayers in which we express gratitude for the little joys of life. Feeling bad makes me thankful when I feel good again. Driving for several months in a car with a broken heater makes me grateful daily for a functional car. God showers our lives with blessings small and large every day—and we can say small and large thank yous.

CHAPTER 17: ASK FOR ADVICE—AND FOLLOW IT

WE CAN BE STUBBORN. We trust our own opinions and thoughts and are suspicious of opposing viewpoints. Even when people have really good reasons, we are extremely reluctant to trust or agree with them. The idea of listening to someone else's advice—giving them the keys to our lives in some small degree—produces a visceral reaction in us. We cling fiercely to our feeling of control.

That's precisely why we need to ask for advice and follow it.

The Biblical Connection

One Bible book in particular emphasizes the need to listen to others. Over and over again Proverbs tells us that true wisdom comes from paying attention to God and to other wise people. The evidence is so extensive that it is worth citing at length.

As the book opens, Solomon explains the origin of wisdom: "*The fear of the LORD is the beginning of knowledge; fools despise wisdom and instruction*"(Prov 1:7). When we have an appropriate fear and respect for God, we can learn. When we don't want anyone to tell us anything, we cannot grow.

Solomon personifies wisdom as a woman who cries out, advertising her wares to all people. "*If you turn at my reproof, behold, I will pour out my spirit to you; I will make my words known to you. Because I have called and you refused to listen, have stretched out my hand and no one has heeded, because you have ignored all my counsel and would have none of my reproof, I also will laugh at your calamity; I will mock when terror strikes you*"(Prov 1:23-26). It is important to note that wisdom is described here as "*reproof*." To grow wise, we must develop an appetite to hear challenging words.

Often in Proverbs that reproof comes from a father. "*A fool despises his father's instruction, but whoever heeds reproof is prudent*"(Prov 15:5). A father gives advice and guidance to his son. Since any good father wants the best for his son, ignoring his advice is tragically unwise.

Our stubbornness has an ironic twist. "*Whoever ignores instruction despises himself, but he who listens to reproof gains intelligence*"(Prov 15:32). We think clinging to our own wisdom is a blessing when we actually are hurting ourselves. It is when we listen to instruction that we grow wise.

Proverbs is written in the tone of a father instructing his son. As if on cue, Solomon's own son ignores all of his dad's advice and proves the point. We spoke earlier about Rehoboam (see chapter 7). When faced with a difficult policy problem, he asks for advice, but

116

doesn't follow it. The biblical author notes at this point that Rehoboam *"abandoned the counsel that the old men gave him and took counsel with the young men who had grown up with him and stood before him"*(1 Kings 12:8).

What Rehoboam does here is particularly helpful because it mirrors a common practice. Asking for advice is not the difficult part. We often want to know what others think. But like Rehoboam, we often ask *with our minds already made up.* We know what we want to hear and we are prepared to accept or discount the advice we received based on whether it matches our already-formed opinion. We deceive ourselves, thinking we are seeking advice when what we are really seeking is confirmation. This is nothing but pride warmed-over.

Why Is This Hard?

Our culture presses us to make our own choices and forge our own destinies. We are taught to follow our dreams and explore our vision for the world. But others may not share our vision. If they are older, we may be afraid that they are locked into a generational perspective we do not share (or that we have rejected). If they are younger, we may be afraid that they don't have the wisdom or experience to understand. Without even considering the content of their advice, we dismiss them on superficial grounds. We easily convince ourselves that no one else can understand our unique circumstances. We devise a million reasons to discount the advice of others.

Sometimes we, like Rehoboam, seek yes-men who will confirm our initial impressions. Rather than helping us see ourselves rightly and correcting our imbalances, these people simply help us to be a more intense version of our own selves. Following others' advice means change—and change is hard.

Advice also <u>introduces a different perspective</u>. We must adopt different priorities and see from a different vantage. This is all very challenging—and it seems easier to just rely on ourselves.

<u>It is much easier to *ask for* advice than to *actually follow* it</u>. So persists the strange practice of seeking lots of opinions, then ignoring them all to do what we want. The advent of the internet has only accelerated this process. We search and read and gather data only to do what we had already planned. At its heart, it is hard to submit ourselves to others' opinions. After all, they only have to talk about while we have to live it.

How Does This Help with Humility?

By definition, asking for advice <u>reveals our inadequacy and ignorance</u>. We need help. We don't know what to do. We can't see the way forward. By asking for advice, we submit ourselves to others' judgment. We trust them and their wisdom. This lowers us.

We also <u>open ourselves up for inspection</u>. How is my parenting? What do you think of my speech? How can I be a better leader? All of these questions are requests for advice, yet all of them humble us because they invite corrective criticism.

It humbles and challenges us to follow advice that goes against our gut. <u>We put ourselves second</u> to others—particularly those who are older—and do what is unnatural.

Practice humility. Ask others for advice. Ask about situations that are stressful and difficult. Ask about how to deal with that co-worker, how to forgive someone, how to pray, and how to be a better husband or wife. Ask about major decisions—that job offer or that crucial conversation. Invite the scrutiny of others and have the courage to hear what others think.

But don't just ask for advice. Follow it. Follow it when it doesn't seem like the best way—if the person who counsels you is wise and godly. Follow it when it's not the way you think about it at all.

Practice humility. Ask for advice—and follow it.

Field Notes

- <u>There are things you don't see</u>. This practice is a struggle for me. Yet when I have asked and taken advice from others, I am impressed by the fact that older, wiser brothers see trouble where I did not. In one particular situation, a brother advised a course of action that I didn't have a strong opinion on. I listened to him about it—and later, I was incredibly thankful I had. He understood how the situation would play out and how others would view it. Even in our wisest moments, others can see things we do not.

- <u>Suspend criticism</u>. It is fine to disagree with advisors, but it is foolish to quickly dismiss their perspectives. I have found myself even losing respect for people who do not immediately think like I do. I would encourage suspension of criticism so that we can take some time to think through and pray over the advice we have received. Otherwise we might end up with deep regret.

CHAPTER 18: SERVE SOMEONE

IN OUR PRIDE, WE EASILY LOSE CONNECTION with others. We worry about our own comfort and become unpleasant when we encounter even minor inconveniences. We grow out of touch with the suffering in the broader world—or when we hear about it, it doesn't affect us at all. Even when tragedy or pain strikes those close to us, we may acknowledge their pain, but then swiftly return to our preoccupation with ourselves. There is little room for us emptying ourselves of ego and meeting others where they are.

Practice humility. Serve someone.

The Biblical Connection

Service is how Jesus teaches his disciples to break the siren song of ambition. *"But whoever would be great among you must be your servant, and whoever would be first among you must be slave of all. For even the Son of Man came not to be served but to serve, and to give his life as a ransom for many"* (Mark 10:43-45). Great disciples are not those who gain great power and influence; they are those who are great servants. Jesus sets himself as an example in this, emphasizing that he did not come to earth to have others serve him.

It may strike us as strange, but Bible authors repeatedly picture the incarnation as Jesus humbling himself to serve. Paul refers to him while teaching humility and thoughtfulness:

> *"Have this mind among yourselves, which is yours in Christ Jesus, who, though he was in the form of God, did not count equality with God a thing to be grasped, but emptied himself, by taking the form of a servant, being born in the likeness of men. And being found in human form, he humbled himself by becoming obedient to the point of death, even death on a cross"*(Phil 2:5-8).

If you are already familiar with this text, I strongly suggest another look with fresh eyes. Jesus was equal with God, yet refused to stubbornly cling to this status. The text pictures him as continually lowering himself—emptying himself, becoming a servant, becoming a man, becoming obedient, and becoming a byword by dying on a cross. There is absolutely no glamor about Jesus' mission. It is all about others. And Paul teaches *us* to *"have this mind."* To be like Jesus, we must lower ourselves to serve.

Paul also cites Jesus' example when encouraging the Corinthians to give to their needy brothers: *"For you know the grace of our Lord Jesus Christ, that though he was rich, yet for your sake he became poor, so that you by his poverty might become rich"*(2 Cor 8:9). Watching Jesus lower himself to bless sinful mankind whets our appetite to follow his footsteps by serving others.

But it is not just Jesus' coming to earth that shows his servant's heart. Jesus is continually serving—talking with and healing the crowds, encouraging and confronting his disciples, and rarely taking any time for himself. The lasting image of the gospels is Jesus—on the night he is betrayed—taking a bowl of water and scrubbing dirt off the feet of his disciples. Even in this remarkably tense moment, he is still thinking about everyone around him.

So it is not surprising that followers of Jesus become servants. Paul illustrates what that means regarding people who are outside Christ:

> "For though I am free from all, I have made myself a servant to all, that I might win more of them. To the Jews I became as a Jew, in order to win Jews. To those under the law I became as one under the law (though not being myself under the law) that I might win those under the law. To those outside the law I became as one outside the law (not being outside the law of God but under the law of Christ) that I might win those outside the law. To the weak I became weak, that I might win the weak. I have become all things to all people, that by all means I might save some" (1 Cor 9:19-22).

Though he is free, he has *made himself* a servant. He wants to serve others, sacrificing parts of his personality to best emphasize what would draw someone to Christ. He can talk law with any Jew. He can talk sports with any Gentile. He can be *"all things to all people"* to win them to Christ. Paul illustrates the heart of a servant: willingly accepting inconvenience, ceding rights, and going above and beyond for the good of others.

Why Is This Hard?

Our self-fixation makes service unnatural. We tend to look at and think about our own problems. To some extent, we must do this; it is part of taking care of our own business and bearing our own load. But when the bulk of our attention, energy, and time is spent on our own pursuits, it is easy to forget that others need our help, care, time, and consideration.

We also have a tendency to really like (and get used to) *being served*. We enjoy being honored. If someone wants to give us things and make our lives nicer, we accept. Who wouldn't want that? Then we begin to look at all relationships—particularly local church relationships—as mercenaries, asking what others are going to do for us. This is a hard mindset to break.

Service is hard because, like Paul, we don't *have* to serve. Paul says "*I have made myself a servant*." It's a choice. That means that we must go against the grain of our nature (and culture) and choose to give instead of receive.

The reality of service is also not glamorous. Service lowers and humiliates us. It usually costs us—our time, money, energy, or the opportunity to do something we enjoy. Very rarely do people appreciate (or even notice) service, so we must be highly motivated to continue. Sometimes we run out of resources and wind up exhausted and frustrated. When we try to tackle a problem or need, our service seems to never be enough to truly make a difference. It is a drop of our lives in a bucket of need.

How Does This Help with Humility?

Paul overtly connects service with humility (Phil 2:3-8). The reason is simple: <u>when we serve, we are not the stars</u>. We are honoring others. We are considering others and deeming them more valuable than ourselves. We are sacrificing for others. We might not be noticed or thanked. All of this will help us toward humility.

When we serve, we <u>restore the proper order</u>. Jesus insists that he "*came not to be served but to serve*"(Mark 10:45). However thankful we may be for Jesus' sacrifice for us, we are missing its import if we think the goal is for us to be continually served. Serving means we are adopting the character of Jesus and putting ourselves back in our proper place. Jesus wants us to think of ourselves as servants (Luke 17:7-10); this will be hard until we decide to actually serve.

Practice humility. Help others without any agenda whatsoever. Meet urgent needs. Be there for people. Encourage someone who is struggling. Follow up. Give money to someone in need. Visit someone who is lonely. Give someone a break: Wash their dishes. Mow their yard. Watch their kids. Fix them some food. Help someone reach their potential. Take on a project that is not about you at all. Invite someone into your social plans. Be a shoulder to cry on. Ask how people are doing.

Practice humility. Serve someone.

Field Notes

- <u>Service is the answer to a number of spiritual ailments</u>. Very often, if we find ourselves consumed with anxiety, wracked by doubt, beset by laziness, discontent and ill-at-ease, *it is because we are not serving others*. Navel-gazing leads to spiritual malaise. Serving is spiritual exercise—it keeps us healthy, strengthens our connections with others, and leaves us far too exhausted to get frustrated with everyone else. When I get down, service picks me up.

- <u>Don't forget to fill up</u>. Service will drain you. It is only natural that when we give and give, we have very little left. Even Jesus had to withdraw himself from the crowds and reconnect with God (Matt 14:13, 22-23). Giving without receiving nourishment for yourself will lead to burnout. Serve others, but don't forget to fill up.

CHAPTER 19: GIVE A SOFT ANSWER

CONFLICT OFTEN BRINGS OUT THE WORST in us. Christian values are instantly jettisoned in favor of self-preservation. Our pride gets involved. Ugly words must be returned. Retaliation seems justified. We easily feel wronged and aggrieved, ready to act in whatever way their behavior has made necessary.

We can practice humility by learning to give a soft answer.

The Biblical Connection

Scripture repeatedly teaches us the value of responding well to others' hostility. *"A soft answer turns away wrath, but a harsh word stirs up anger"*(Prov 15:1). The *"answer"* part of the verse stresses that we are responding to something someone else has done or said. Sometimes these are actual wrongs; more often they are perceived. Occasionally we are tempted to lash out in a way far out of proportion to the situation. A *"soft answer"* is a way we calm the situation instead of escalating it. Yet when we offer a *"harsh word,"* we add fuel to the fire.

A couple of proverbs link a soft answer to patience. *"With patience a ruler may be persuaded, and a soft tongue will break a bone"*(Prov 25:15). We can often persuade even powerful people if we are persistent and careful in our speech. His resistance may be strong, like a bone, but our soft answer can overcome it. *"A hot-tempered man stirs up strife, but he who is slow to anger quiets contention"*(Prov 15:18). Patience here is shown in refusing to be easily angered, preferring instead to speak kindly and keep peace.

The Bible then shows us the soft answer/harsh word contrast in living color. In the time of the judges, Gideon fights against Midian. After the victory, some of his countrymen confront him for not calling on them to help in the battle:

> *"'What is this that you have done to us, not to call us when you went to fight against Midian?' And they accused him fiercely. And he said to them, 'What have I done now in comparison with you? Is not the gleaning of the grapes of Ephraim better than the grape harvest of Abiezer? God has given into your hands the princes of Midian, Oreb and Zeeb. What have I been able to do in comparison with you?' Then their anger against him subsided when he said this"(Judges 8:1-3).*

Gideon gives a soft answer to the Ephraimites. He praises the good they have done and lowers himself in the process. He speaks kindly to them—even though he easily could have barked back. As a result, they calm down.

A few years later, Jephthah is judge instead of Gideon. These same Ephraimites get angry with him about not calling them to help in the battle. Note Jephthah's answer:

"'Why did you cross over to fight against the Ammonites and did not call us to go with you? We will burn your house over you with fire.' And Jephthah said to them, 'I and my people had a great dispute with the Ammonites, and when I called you, you did not save me from their hand. And when I saw that you would not save me, I took my life in my hand and crossed over against the Ammonites, and the LORD gave them into my hand. Why then have you come up to me this day to fight against me?' Then Jephthah gathered all the men of Gilead and fought with Ephraim"(Judges 12:1-4).

Jephthah, meanwhile, provokes further conflict with a harsh response to the accusations. Both Gideon and Jephthah are wrongfully confronted, yet Gideon's soft answer averts war. Jephthah shows the way our words can dramatically escalate conflicts.

David has a similar experience. After watching over the shepherds of Nabal, a rich landowner, David asks him to give some food to his servants. *"And Nabal answered David's servants, 'Who is David? Who is the son of Jesse? There are many servants these days who are breaking away from their masters. Shall I take my bread and my water and my meat that I have killed for my shearers and give it to men who come from I do not know where?"*(1 Sam 25:10-11). This is a harsh answer. David is angry and begins to advance on Nabal with his men. Yet Abigail, Nabal's wife, rushes out to David and pleads with him, apologizing for her husband, bringing presents and reasoning with him. Abigail brings a soft answer and prevents disaster.

Scripture also acknowledges that there will be times when—no matter how sweetly we talk—conflict is inevitable. *"Repay no one evil for evil, but give thought to do what is honorable in the sight of all. If possible, so far as it depends on you, live peaceably with all"* (Rom 12:17-18). God wants us to live at peace with all—and that will involve abandoning our own attempts at revenge. It will include keeping our tongue still, even when we've been wronged. Certainly there are times when others will insist on conflict, but God tells us repeatedly that most conflict is avoidable if we are willing to give a soft answer.

Why Is This Hard?

Soft answers are hard because <u>we want so desperately to fire back</u>. When others harm us, assault us verbally, or attempt to provoke us, we are naturally defensive. We must respond and stand up for ourselves! Set them straight! Don't let them walk all over you!

We also have a tendency to <u>always feel justified in our responses to others</u>. Any word, action, look, or tone of voice that we interpret to be an attack against us makes retaliation valid. We are much less likely to look critically at our own words and actions when we feel that we have been wronged. They started it!

Soft answers are also hard because <u>we feel angry and embarrassed</u>. Will we lose face? What do others think? Are we going to let ourselves be talked to that way? These are not our best emotional states to be thoughtful and careful.

How Does This Help with Humility?

When we give a soft answer, <u>we are enduring the wrong</u>. We are de-escalating the conflict. We lower ourselves by absorbing whatever minor indignities have been committed against us.

Personally, I struggle with giving soft answers because when I am engaged in a verbal argument, *I want to win*. <u>Soft answers show that we value resolving (or avoiding) the conflict more than we do advancing our own agenda</u>. We are actively pushing our goals, thoughts, and agendas into the background so that we can seek peace together.

Soft answers also bring up a series of very helpful questions: Why do I not want to allow this person to be right in this situation? What is our common ground? What does God want in this situation? Am I really responding to this in the best way? Choosing to give a soft answer <u>opens our horizons to consider other dimensions of the situation</u>.

Practice humility. Many conflicts can be defused if we can get our egos out of the way. Discipline your mouth and response. Stop yourself when you want to respond in anger or frustration. Keep that zinger in your back pocket.

Practice humility. Give a soft answer.

Field Notes

- <u>Wait a beat</u>. All of us have an instinctive response when others attack. It usually involves clapping back. I find it helpful to take a breath and think through before I respond in a way that will be difficult to take back. Impulsive answers are not thoughtful.

- <u>Think about areas of agreement</u>. One of my favorite ways to give soft answers is to take the other person's contention and take it to an area that I know we agree on. Where their words separate us, I want my words to bring us back together. We are more likely to be at peace when we are moving in the same direction.

CHAPTER 20: LET IT GO

A MERICANS ARE A PEOPLE OF OUTRAGE. We find ways to get offended and upset daily—from poor service at a restaurant to upsetting political developments. We rally and fuss and get angry. We have lost the virtue and wisdom in learning to get over the minor inconveniences and frustration common to all people.

We desperately need to learn to let things go.

The Biblical Connection

As Jesus preaches in a region outside of Israel, a Canaanite woman approaches him to get him to cast a demon out of her daughter. First Jesus ignores her (Matt 15:23). When the disciples ask him to send her away, he says, "*I was sent only to the lost sheep of the house of Israel*"(Matt 15:24). She kneels and begs for his help and he blithely tells her, "*It is not right to take the children's bread and throw it to the dogs*"(Matt 15:26), further insulting her. "*She said, 'Yes, Lord, yet even the dogs eat the crumbs that fall from their masters' table*"(Matt 15:27). Jesus is deeply impressed by her faith and heals her daughter instantly.

This woman has several opportunities to be deeply offended. Jesus ignores her, excludes her, and insults her. She refuses to let these experiences keep her from the blessing she seeks for her daughter. Surely she has her thoughts about Jesus' treatment of her, but she lets it go. Looking back on it, it seems that Jesus knows that her perseverance will be shown by her willingness to swallow her pride. He acts to draw out her humility.

Paul and Barnabas, though good friends and co-workers, have a strong disagreement. John Mark, Barnabas' cousin, accompanied them on their first missionary journey but returned home early (Acts 13:13). As they plan for their second journey, Barnabas wants to bring John Mark again. Paul refuses, still smarting that John Mark abandoned them before. They have a *"sharp disagreement"*(Acts 15:39) and decide to go their separate ways. What is interesting is that Paul seems to come around on John Mark. Later in his life, he mentions him as someone to be welcomed (Col 4:10) and asks Timothy to *"get Mark and bring him with you, for he is very useful to me for ministry"*(2 Tim 4:11). Paul is frustrated by John Mark, but he learns to let it go.

Sometimes it is major things that we must learn to let go. In a fit of jealousy, Joseph's brothers sell him into slavery. He suffers and labors in Egypt. After a number of years, Joseph advances and becomes second in the land. He is reunited with his brothers. They are terrified he still holds a grudge, yet Joseph has let it go. *"As for you, you meant evil against me, but God meant it for good, to bring it about that many people should be kept alive, as they are today. So do not fear; I will provide for you and your little ones"*(Gen 50:20-21). Joseph sees how God has woven their evil deed into good—blessing, saving, and fulfilling his promises.

The Bible says a lot about forgiveness. Jesus particularly stresses our need to pass God's forgiveness on to others (Matt 18:21-35, Luke 17:3-4, Matt 6:12-15). We have questions and concerns about that. Forgiveness is not about ignoring sin. It does not mean that the other person "got away with it." Forgiveness is about the steadfast determination to not let other people's evil stick in our hearts, corrupting and embittering us.

But more than just sin, a lot of the hurts we experience are personal slights, ugliness, and grudges. Some of these things never get aired publicly. They are not headline sins, just the bumps and bruises of everyday life. We practice humility by learning to let it go.

Why Is This Hard?

It's hard to let it go because <u>we're hurt and we're mad</u>! Letting it go feels like we're saying that our emotions don't matter.

Sometimes <u>we're unsure just exactly *how* we let it go</u>. Do we need to talk to them? Jesus teaches us to resolve these hostilities quickly: *"So if you are offering your gift at the altar and there remember that your brother has something against you, leave your gift there before the altar and go. First be reconciled to your brother, and then come and offer your gift"* (Matt 5:23-24). Some things are troubling and upsetting and reach the level where we need to go meet with them. Sometimes there are slights that we can immediately ignore and move on. Sometimes it's hard to know which course is appropriate.

It is clear from the passage just cited that Jesus wants us to deal with the problem, yet <u>our tendency is to shove it down and ignore it</u>. Sometimes we gossip about it with others. We rehearse it in our minds, poking the bruise. We like to do everything *but* proactively resolve the issue and find peace.

As we grow more and more bitter, letting things go becomes harder and harder. <u>We lose objectivity</u>. We get so angry that we can't hear reason. We cling more tightly to our pain and sense of rightness.

There is pride here.

How Does This Help with Humility?

Paul teaches us to "*never avenge yourselves, but leave it to the wrath of God, for it is written, 'Vengeance is mine, I will repay, says the Lord'*" (Rom 12:19). <u>When we forfeit vengeance and give room for God to be God, we lower ourselves</u>. We are no longer in the driver's seat. God will do the repaying, not us. We leave it to him.

When we let things go, <u>we give up our right to condescend to those who have hurt us</u>. We cede our right to be angry. We refuse to remain victims. We declare ourselves on equal footing with the person who has hurt, inconvenienced, or upset us. It's over. We have let it go.

There is also humility in submitting ourselves to the will of God, <u>trusting the vengeance God will bring</u>. If there are any scores that need to be settled, God is perfectly capable of handling that. He doesn't need me to hang on to those offenses for him and he doesn't need my help with setting others right.

Pride sometimes takes the form of assuming that our wounds are worse than everyone else's. Our pain is more painful. Our injustices are more unjust. No one can understand. Letting it go reminds us that <u>we are no different than any other person</u>—and that God's expectations apply equally to us.

Letting things go can also <u>bless others</u>. We often don't realize it when we have been hurt, but when we hold on to our hurts, we keep alive a bad thing someone else has done. We remind them— and everyone who talks with us—of their worst chapters. When we let it go, we gain humility by declaring that their need to move on matters to us too.

Letting it go <u>frees us up to see purpose in the things that have happened to us</u>. Joseph is able to see God at work, despite the fact that he has been hurt: *"As for you, you meant evil against me, but God meant it for good"*(Gen 50:20). God's story doesn't stop because we have been offended or upset. God can often use that to refine us, bless others, and achieve his purposes. Finding our place in God's story is a step toward humility.

Practice humility. Live forward, not in the past. Resolve to stop brooding over the hurts and disappointments of yesterday. Don't be offended easily. Don't keep a list of all the ways others have upset and frustrated you. Find opportunities and reasons to get over it and move on.

Practice humility. Let it go.

Field Notes

- <u>Don't keep bringing it up</u>. When I have been hurt, I am tempted to tell my woeful story to everyone I encounter. I have even trotted it out when others are expressing *their* hurts to me—as if it is some kind of suffering contest. This isn't helpful—for them or me. When I keep living in the past and referring to all my hurts, I keep alive their power over me. I don't mean that there is not a place to honestly retell our stories, but that our fixation with past hurts is often unhealthy. If we have to keep bringing it up, it signals that our hurt still holds a tremendous power over us—and that we need to let it go.

- <u>It's worth the trouble</u>. There is such freedom when we let things go that it is worth the inconvenience of having to sort out old issues. We may need to have some conversations about past clashes—or even confess our role in ancient hurts. As one who has gone through these processes, I can say with confidence that it is worth the trouble to work it out and let it go.

CHAPTER 21: DEFLECT A COMPLIMENT

WHEN WE ARE COMPLIMENTED, we feel a strange blend of pride, satisfaction, validation, and a desire to appear gracious and humble. It is a pivotal moment. We experience an inner battle between humbly receiving praise and feeding a hungry ego. How do we keep the natural need for feedback balanced with our insatiable desire for respect and acceptance?

In moments of pride, we easily deflect criticism and take every compliment to heart. This is precisely backward, keeping us from learning anything from others' feedback while expanding our egos.

It will help us toward humility to learn to deflect compliments.

The Biblical Connection

The biblical record contains several people whom God empowers to do his work. They very often respond to praise of their powers by deflecting compliments and emphasizing that it is God who is responsible.

When Joseph is a prisoner in Egypt, Pharaoh summons him to interpret his dreams. *"And Pharaoh said to Joseph, 'I have had a dream, and there is no one who can interpret it. I have heard it said of you that when you hear a dream you can interpret it.' Joseph answered Pharaoh, 'It is not in me; God will give Pharaoh a favorable answer'"*(Gen 41:15-16). Joseph refuses to take credit for any interpretations here; he deflects compliments to God.

Daniel is also summoned by a king to interpret a dream. When Nebuchadnezzar asks him if he can tell him the dream and its interpretation, Daniel is very clear: *"No wise men, enchanters, magicians, or astrologers can show to the king the mystery that the king has asked, but there is a God in heaven who reveals mysteries"*(Dan 2:27-28). A moment later he adds (in case there has been any misunderstanding in the last minute or so) this: *"But as for me, this mystery has been revealed to me, not because of any wisdom that I have more than all the living, but in order that the interpretation may be made known to the king, and that you may know the thoughts of your mind"*(Dan 2:30). Daniel insists that he is not super-smart. This is about God. God reveals; he just happens to have revealed this to Daniel.

Peter and John heal a lame man by the temple, which causes the crowds to be amazed. Yet Peter directs their attention away from himself: *"Men of Israel, why do you wonder at this, or why do you stare at us, as though by our own power or piety we have made him walk?"*(Acts 3:12). This is about God. This same Peter will refuse the worship of Cornelius: *"Stand up; I too am a man"*(Acts 10:26).

The apostles seem particularly sensitive about this treatment. They take pains so that *"your faith might not rest in the wisdom of men but in the power of God"* (1 Cor 2:5). Paul says this about himself: *"For I am the least of the apostles, unworthy to be called an apostle, because I persecuted the church of God. But by the grace of God I am what I am, and his grace toward me was not in vain"* (1 Cor 15:9-10). Whatever compliments others would want to pay him, Paul insists that God's grace is what deserves praise here. He even denies that he is sufficient for *his part* in the work of Christ (2 Cor 3:5-6). All the credit goes to God.

Why Is This Hard?

Deflecting compliments is hard because <u>we like praise, respect, and flattery</u>. It makes us feel good and we feel validated when we receive it. Refusing to receive it seems ungrateful and pointless.

Often deflecting compliments is hard because <u>we feel like we deserve them</u>. We genuinely feel that we are responsible for the hard work, brilliant ideas, and success we have experienced. When others praise us, we are internally nodding our heads. "You're right," we are thinking, "I *am* awesome!" There is pride here.

We sometimes lapse into a <u>performer/audience mentality</u>. Our work, our parenting, our social persona—are really about us acting on a stage while others watch. When we succeed, it is only natural for the audience to applaud—and for the performers to take a bow. When we feel that others are constantly evaluating us, it is hard to deflect their praise.

Personally, I find it challenging to <u>differentiate between honest feedback and praise that can feed my ego</u>. We all need to hear from others about their opinions of the things we are doing and saying— and we always want that feedback to be positive. When all feedback is negative, I tend to dismiss it. When it is all positive, I tend to gloat. In my experience, too many compliments is like eating too much candy: it tastes nice, but leaves you feeling empty.

Deflecting compliments is also often <u>awkward</u>. When someone praises us and we try to pass that credit on to someone else, it sounds like we are arguing with them. "Thanks for the work you did on that project." "Actually, there were several of us who did it." These exchanges can sound hostile—or as if we are refusing the compliment—or as if we are correcting them. In fact, they may feel that they must insist that *we* did it—and we must insist that *God* did it or that *others* were really important. We may have to learn a new skill here to gain the humility we're seeking—the art of the graceful deflection.

How Does This Help with Humility?

Deflecting humbles us because <u>it gives God praise instead of ourselves</u>. Who is truly, ultimately responsible? We can always find ways to praise God. If we are successful, God has given us the mind, tools, opportunities, health, and time to achieve. If we are skilled, God has given us talents. If we are sociable, God has blessed us with relationships. *"Every good gift and every perfect gift is from above, coming down from the Father of lights with whom there is no variation or shadow due to change"*(James 1:17). Deflecting compliments merely acknowledges that there is a greater source for those things others want to praise us for. Humility takes something that might lead to pride for us and chooses to praise God.

This tool also <u>forces us to ask some questions of ourselves</u>: Just what part of this did *I* do? How much of this was beyond my control? How can I thank God for the good that is happening?

We can also deflect compliments to other people. Very rarely is any achievement solely our own doing. People have contributed in many ways to our development and successes. It is always appropriate to remind those who would praise us that <u>we are really beneficiaries of the efforts and sacrifices of many people</u>. This lowers us.

The power of deflection is in the fact that it changes our self-estimation and puts that change into *words*. <u>We express humility by actively not expressing pride</u>. While we would easily acknowledge that God's blessings and others' help contribute to our successes, deflecting compliments trains us to seek out these truths rather than feed our egos.

Practice humility. Be gracious and kind to others. Find a way to deflect to others and to God. Be thankful, giving praise rather than receiving it.

Practice humility. Deflect a compliment.

Field Notes

- <u>Test out some expressions</u>. It is a real challenge to find ways to deflect compliments that sound natural. Test out expressions to find what sounds right in your mouth: "Thank you for your kind words, but..." or "You know who's really responsible?..." or "Thank you, I feel truly blessed" or "You are so kind to encourage me. Thanks for your thoughtfulness." Show appreciation for the encouragement, but push it onward.

CHAPTER 22: WORSHIP

WORSHIP IS THE ACT OF PRAISING GOD by saying good things about him and by doing certain acts that honor him. It has been a part of man's life and makeup from the beginning — or at least Cain and Abel. Man is hardwired to worship. But there is more here than simply fulfilling our purpose; worship humbles us. Taking the time and effort to worship God refocuses our attention toward something more positive than ourselves.

One of the greatest steps we will ever take toward humility is sincerely worshipping God.

The Biblical Connection

Worship is all over the pages of the Bible. Long before the Law of Moses, the patriarchs build altars on which to sacrifice animals to honor God (Gen 12:7-8; 33:20). Moses' Law codifies worship for Israel, setting up the priests, regulating sacrifices, establishing feast days, and giving rules for the tabernacle/temple. For Christians, the New Testament adds the unique feast of the Lord's Supper (1 Cor 11:17-34) and moves away from the priestly system. Christian worship involves singing, prayer, and presentation of the word in various forms.

But what is worship? It is expressing the greatness of God and giving him and his things positive attention. It is bowing ourselves before him. *"Oh come, let us worship and bow down; let us kneel before the LORD, our Maker! For he is our God, and we are the people of his pasture, and the sheep of his hand"* (Psalm 95:6-7). In worship, we *kneel before* God, giving our praise and our allegiance to him. We express gratitude and a desire to serve.

This worship naturally leads toward humility. David begins a psalm with *"O LORD, our Lord, how majestic is your name in all the earth"* and then proceeds to muse on how God has placed man among his creation: *"When I look at the heavens, the work of your fingers, the moon and the stars, which you have set in place, what is man that you are mindful of him, and the son of man that you care for him?"* (Psalm 8:1, 3-4). Praising God for his creative work naturally leads David to express his awe that God would think so much of people. As we elevate God, we lower ourselves.

In a very tender scene, God promises David that he will establish his family dynasty forever. *"Then King David went in and sat before the LORD and said, 'Who am I, O Lord GOD, and what is my house, that you have brought me thus far? And yet this was a small thing in your eyes, O Lord GOD'"* (2 Sam 7:18-19). David is so overwhelmed and grateful that he enters the place of worship and prays in shock to God: Who am I, that you would do this for me?

What is man—that you have so honored him? Who am I—that you have made these promises to me? This is the posture of biblical worship.

Scripture also places an emphasis on the fact that when we worship, we offer something. In describing the feasts, God declares,

"None shall appear before me empty-handed"(Ex 23:15). David insists, *"I will not offer burnt offerings to the LORD my God that cost me nothing"*(2 Sam 24:24). Jews brought animals to offer—the best of herds and flocks—and in their worship they gave these things up to God to take away sin or to show their devotion. Paul encourages Christians to *"present your bodies as a living sacrifice, holy and acceptable to God, which is your spiritual worship"*(Rom 12:1). We offer ourselves fully to God—body, heart, money, time, and energy. This is part of worship.

But we must always keep in mind that worship is not something God needs; it is something *we* need. *"The God who made the world and everything in it, being Lord of heaven and earth, does not live in temples made by man, nor is he served by human hands, as though he needed anything, since he himself gives to all mankind life and breath and everything"*(Acts 17:24-25). God is not dependent on our worship and sacrifices. He will be just fine whether we worship him or not. *But we will not be the same.* Worship refocuses us, reminds us of divine priorities, gives us an outlet for our gratitude, and demands that we reverence things that are not directly connected with our egos.

Why Is This Hard?

The main obstacle to worship in our time is our relentless focus on entertainment. Worshipping God is just not as exciting as whatever games, movies, or hobbies we are used to consuming. Those things are tailored to draw our interest and please us. Worship is far different. It does not promise entertainment or gratification. It promises humility, truth, and an alternative perspective. It challenges us. If we only see such things through the lens of whether they are boring or entertaining, we will find true worship difficult.

Worship is hard because <u>we like being the center of attention</u>. Even if we don't want to be noticed, we still enjoy having our desires met and our happiness a priority. Worship turns this on its head. It challenges us to make *God* the center of *our* attention.

Worship is also hard because <u>we prefer our own perspective</u>. Interacting with God means that we will be challenged to think differently about our lives and our choices. He will broaden our perspective so that we see the value in all people (not just ourselves), the long-term view of life (not just immediate pleasure), and the true devastation of our sin. It's much simpler for us to just stay in our own bubble.

Worship is a challenge because <u>it's voluntary</u>. No one forces us to do it. We can just as easily go through our days ignoring God and others—and there are no voices from heaven correcting us. Even when we do worship, we can just go through the motions without allowing it to touch our hearts. This only increases the difficulty.

How Does This Help with Humility?

Eugene Peterson defines worship this way:

> *"Worship is the strategy by which we interrupt our preoccupation with ourselves and attend to the presence of God. It's the time and place that we assign for deliberate attentiveness to God...because our self-importance is so insidiously relentless that if we don't deliberately interrupt ourselves regularly, we have no*

chance of attending to him at all in other times and other places"[9]

Peterson highlights how worship humbles us: stopping us from fixating on ourselves, giving our attention to God, and developing a habit for interruption of our tendency to self-absorption. God is praised, spoken about, obeyed, meditated on, understood, and emphasized. Authentic worship will humble us.

In worship, <u>we are giving praise, not receiving it</u>. Worship should make us feel good, but in a different way than when we receive honor from others. We do not leave worship experiences — prayer, singing, meditation, reading Scripture, fasting, and the like — with the sensation that we are great. Worship reminds us that we have the ability to praise others — that in fact, we were made to do this — and that God is the most praiseworthy being there is.

In worship <u>we are given perspective, not giving it</u>. Very often Scripture broadens our perspective by showing us the world from God's viewpoint. Job learns that there is more to the world than his personal grievances. Revelation shows suffering Christians that while chaos abounds on earth, God remains on his heavenly throne, fully in charge. While we certainly can express our own concerns and thoughts to God in worship, we do not aim to change God's mind. God changes ours.

In worship, <u>we come to learn, not to teach</u>. We do not approach God to correct him, but to be corrected and challenged and improved. Worship reverses our tendency to give our opinions and

---

[9] Peterson, *Leap Over a Wall*, cited in Yancey, p. 127.

tell others what we think. As we encounter God, we remember that *he* is the one with the knowledge, not us. We are not elevated above others; instead, we sit together at the feet of Jesus to listen and learn.

Practice humility. Set aside time to worship God. Involve yourself in the worship of a local church. Take time to listen to prepared Bible studies in which you connect to God through his word. Pray. Sing spiritual songs of praise. Read the Bible yourself. Meditate on the nature of God or a part of his word. Interrupt your schedule and worship God.

Practice humility. Worship.

Field Notes

- <u>Focus takes practice</u>. There is an intensity in worship that is hard to maintain. We are setting our attention on a being we cannot see and concepts that are nebulous. We will get distracted and occasionally bored, but this does not mean that we are "bad" at worship or that there is no value in it. It means that we need the discipline of continual practice to train our focus to remain on God and his things.

- <u>Mean what you say</u>. There is a strong temptation in worship to rely on rote phrases and ideas. Jesus warns us against praying with *"empty phrases"*(Matt 6:7). The danger is that when we repeat the words and thoughts of others, they hold little meaning for us. My rule of thumb is that in worship, I will try my hardest to mean everything I say. I will mean what I pray, sing, read and discuss, teach, and say to encourage. I may struggle with the precise wording—and I may even have to be silent to find words and thoughts that are meaningful—but I will not resort to rote phrases and ideas because God deserves more from me.

CHAPTER 23: HOLD YOUR TONGUE

WE TALK A LOT. Sometimes that's because we feel an urgency to express our thoughts and ideas. If we don't speak, someone else will! They will outshine us. They will take the credit. But if we do speak, we can enlighten them, sharing our wisdom and gaining their respect. Even when we are well aware of the dangers that accompany our talking, we plunge headlong anyway.

Humility comes when we practice holding our tongues.

The Biblical Connection

Scripture paints speech as a self-discipline issue. *"If anyone thinks he is religious and does not bridle his tongue but deceives his heart, this person's religion is useless"*(James 1:26). *"Bridle"* is an intriguing word that suggests both limiting and harnessing the power of the tongue for maximum effectiveness. Like all self-discipline issues, it begins with the simple ability to tell ourselves "no" when our natural instinct is to speak out. James implies that our speech should be carefully calculated.

The Proverbs particularly highlight the danger of talking too much. *"When words are many, transgression is not lacking, but whoever restrains his lips is prudent"*(Prov 10:19). We don't have to talk to sin, but lots of sin involves talking. Solomon advises restraint.

"Whoever keeps his mouth and his tongue keeps himself out of trouble"(Prov 21:23). Guarding our speech guards us from trouble. We have all experienced the inverse of this idea—our words getting us into trouble—but we often fail to attempt the solution. Holding our tongues will bless us.

"Whoever restrains his words has knowledge, and he who has a cool spirit is a man of understanding"(Prov 17:27). Here the writer links holding our tongues and having a *"cool spirit"*—meaning a calm, even-tempered disposition. Often our initial response to a person or situation is an overreaction. We get angry or annoyed or offended or hurt or frustrated and we speak out of our emotion. We usually regret this. Holding our tongue will help us react appropriately.

One proverb speaks to a particular setting in which holding our tongue is essential: *"If one gives an answer before he hears, it is his folly and shame"*(Prov 18:13). Sometimes we think we already know what someone is going to say or how a situation is going to play out. Like a chess player looking two moves ahead, we correct the problem as we see it—only to discover that we have completely misread the situation and misunderstood the person. We give answers before we hear. While they are talking, we are merely rehearsing mentally what we are going to say when they finally finish. The proverb reminds us that there is a place for listening patiently to others. Holding our tongue will keep us from jumping the conversational gun.

The Bible also records a story in which holding the tongue is a mercy. When Job endures the loss of his children, wealth, and health in rapid succession, his friends come to him. "*And they sat with him on the ground seven days and seven nights, and no one spoke a word to him, for they saw that his suffering was very great*" (Job 2:13). These friends have a lot to say (they will speak a *lot* in the book of Job!), yet here holding their tongues helps them comfort Job. They honor him by their silence. It is when they begin to speak—and accuse Job of wrong—that he calls them "*miserable comforters*" (Job 16:2). Sometimes it is better to say nothing.

Why Is This Hard?

Since holding our tongue is a self-control issue, we often struggle with fighting the <u>impulse to immediately say whatever we are thinking or feeling</u>. While a lot of our impulses—such as buying things or abusing substances—require some effort and forethought, speaking off the cuff is always possible and easy. It is holding our tongues that is hard.

We have thoughts and opinions. Because they are ours, we naturally think that they are the best thoughts and opinions. <u>We want to share them</u>. Often we sincerely believe our words will help others (like Job's friends), so we speak freely. Almost everyone wants their time in the conversational spotlight, seeking validation, acceptance, respect, and attention from others. Holding our tongues means forgoing all of these things in pursuit of something much more nebulous. That's hard.

Sometimes our speech is merely <u>filling the vacuum</u> in a conversation. I cannot count the number of times I have said something foolish, critical, or sinful simply because I ran out of things to say and wanted to cover the awkwardness of silence. I didn't mean to use my tongue that way, but I was more afraid of the disapproval of others than careful of keeping the bridle on my tongue. Holding our tongues is hard because we are afraid it will hinder us pursuing relationships with others.

How Does This Help with Humility?

Choosing silence <u>lowers our estimation of ourselves</u>. When we make silence our default setting instead of speaking, we begin to feel the need to *justify our speaking rather than assuming it is warranted.* Why must we speak? Why do we think so highly of our thoughts and words? Why must we give our unsolicited opinions? These are sobering questions.

Going without speaking for a while will also help us <u>appreciate the blessing of communication and learn to choose our words more wisely</u>. Like fasting, we see the gift more clearly when we do without it. We are humbled by seeing that the world gets along just fine without our input and that our instinct to throw words at a problem doesn't always help.

Silence also helps us remember that <u>we don't have all the answers</u>. If we are willing to admit that we don't know (see chapter 3), then we won't have much to say. But we have all been in situations where we felt tempted to talk above our heads. The discipline of silence will remind us that if we don't have anything helpful to add to a situation, holding our tongues is an option.

Choosing silence also <u>helps us think of others more than ourselves</u>. "*Do nothing from selfish ambition or conceit, but in humility count others more significant than yourselves*"(Phil 2:3). If we truly want to count others as more significant than ourselves, we must be willing to listen to them. We seek to know their thoughts, concerns, impressions, and opinions—even if we think we know better.

Holding our tongues means <u>allowing *others* to steer the conversation</u>. We might not talk about our favorite topics. We may not be able to tell our favorite anecdotes. We might allow them to vent about a frustrating situation—which will keep *us* from venting. All of this is training in humility.

Silence also <u>opens us up to truly listen to others</u>. "*Let every person be quick to hear, slow to speak, slow to anger*"(James 1:19). We can only be quick to hear if we are slow to speak. We must listen and consider. It is tempting to rush through what others have to say. We don't consider what they are expressing. We don't think about them much at all, except as the target of our words. Holding our tongue slows down this entire process so that we can truly hear. We can listen for their needs, their spiritual state, their passions, and their disappointments. We honor them by showing them we truly long to get to know them. We lower ourselves.

Practice humility. Become a better listener. Reserve your thoughts and opinions for when they are asked. Let others steer conversations. Ask questions and hold back your own answers. Be careful what you say and how much you say. Consciously limit your number of words.

Practice humility. Hold your tongue.

Field Notes

- <u>Don't be offended when others don't notice</u>. Silence is not always appreciated or even noticed. I tried to hold my tongue for most of a day, carefully weighing my words and allowing others to have the spotlight. My wife didn't even notice! This was even more humiliating. I realized then that all my words, which I had imagined were pearls of wisdom and brilliance, added very little to others. They didn't even miss them! This is good training in humility.

CHAPTER 24: REMEMBER YOUR ROOTS

W E ALL COME FROM SOMEWHERE. There are people who knew us as less than the fully-formed adults we are today. We all have a past that involves the shamelessness of babyhood and the cringeworthy moments of adolescence. Pride can make us want to brush those memories and relationships aside because they embarrass and humiliate us.

We all have a spiritual past too—acts and words we wish we could erase. These are more than mere immaturity; they speak of rebellion. These are scenes that we are still ashamed of. They haunt us and make us hang our heads. Pride can make us want to move on from such behaviors and ignore them.

Remembering our roots will humble us.

The Biblical Connection

Scripture makes this connection in both physical and spiritual arenas. When Moses instructs the children of Israel about their treatment of slaves, he expects their fairness and gentleness to be helped by memories of their own experience in slavery. *"You shall furnish him liberally out of your flock, out of your threshing floor, and out of your winepress. As the LORD your God has blessed you, you shall give to him. You shall remember that you were a slave in the land of Egypt and the LORD your God redeemed you; therefore I command you this today"*(Deut 15:14-15). Moses reminds them of their roots to keep them from feeling that they are better than those who are their servants. We treat others differently when we remember that we have been where they are.

Many of the first generation of Christians in the New Testament era are Gentiles—people who previously had no knowledge of Jehovah God and little sense of moral discipline. Paul wants these people to remember that this is where they come from. *"Therefore remember that at one time you Gentiles in the flesh, called 'the uncircumcision' by what is called the circumcision, which is made in the flesh by hands—remember that you were at that time separated from Christ, alienated from the commonwealth of Israel and strangers to the covenants of promise, having no hope and without God in the world"*(Eph 2:11-12). They need to remember because it gives them a deeper sense of how far they have come—from a godless people to a part of his family. They need to remember their former hopelessness and desperation because it will help them appreciate what has been done for them.

Paul directly connects this to humility. He describes God's people as a great olive tree. Previously, it held only the natural branches (the Jews), but now God has grafted in wild branches (the Gentiles) to make one tree out of the two. *"Then you will say, 'Branches were broken off so that I might be grafted in.' That is true. They were broken off because of their unbelief, but you stand fast through faith. So do not become proud, but fear. For if God did not spare the natural branches, neither will he spare you"*(Rom 11:19-21). Rather than hardening into pride, Paul intends for this reminder of their roots to motivate Gentile believers. Looking back breeds gratitude and loyalty.

This also works on a personal level. Paul remains deeply aware of his roots: *"I thank him who has given me strength, Christ Jesus our Lord, because he judged me faithful, appointing me to his service, though formerly I was a blasphemer, persecutor, and insolent opponent. But I received mercy because I had acted ignorantly in unbelief. And the grace of our Lord overflowed for me with the faith and love that are in Christ Jesus"*(1 Tim 1:12-14). Paul makes clear that this is who he *used to be* (*"formerly I was"*), but it is a part of his story. He has a past and he owns it. Yet he has been saved from that past by the grace of Jesus. Remembering our roots leaves us humbled and thankful.

Why Is This Hard?

Remembering our roots is challenging because <u>we want to move on</u>. We are ashamed and embarrassed at what we have done. These are our worst moments. If we have been saved from them, we want to live in that relief, not go back to the pain. Every reference to those things stings.

<u>We also often want to move on from many parts of our childhood</u>. We want to be judged by the person we are *now*, not the person who did or said immature, embarrassing things. Or perhaps

we want to be known for our own virtues rather than those of our family. In all of it, our desire for a clean slate means we hesitate to remember.

Remembering our roots is hard because <u>we struggle with balancing the past and the present</u>. We know that it is unhealthy to continually live in the past—whether we are celebrating glory days or reliving old failures. Yet it is also unhealthy to willfully forget the past and the lessons it holds for us. Too much focus on the past can leave us overwhelmed and regretful; too much focus on the present can leave us proud.

People also generally have <u>short memories</u>. We quickly adjust to changes in our lives and become accustomed to wherever we are. Remembering our roots will mean consciously focusing on old, unpleasant memories when we don't have to.

How Does This Help with Humility?

Remembering our own sin makes it very hard for us to <u>condescend to others</u>. We are well aware of what it is like to carry guilt around. We know what it is to be slaves to sin, unable to make the changes that we feel are necessary. We have been embarrassed and regretful. So when we see others who have made life-altering mistakes, we have compassion. We are not above it. When we see others lashing out in anger or hurt, we get it. Staying in touch with our spiritual roots lowers us so that we understand that we are just like all other people.

Remembering our physical roots—our youth, raising, and mistakes of immaturity—helps us here too. When we recall that we have been foolish, ignorant children—physically and emotionally fragile—it <u>keeps us from feeling that we are superior to others.</u> We have been weak, needy, poor, and helpless. We have been completely dependent on others to care for and protect us. With these thoughts, it is natural for us to be more patient with others who are weak, needy, poor, and helpless. We relate to them and have common ground. We give advice and comfort not as superiors, but as equals.

Remembering our roots also takes us down an important path of <u>acknowledging the influence of others</u>. We are the product of a great number of people who have taken an interest in our betterment and growth. It is extremely likely that each of us has had people who cared for us physically throughout our childhood. We have also had people who influenced us toward good things and away from bad. Someone introduced the gospel to us so that we could know about the life-changing power of Jesus for ourselves. Going back to our roots highlights the ways that others have altered our path—some for the worse, but many for the better. We are left grateful to them for all the ways they have helped us.

Looking at our history—when done properly—<u>leads to us praising God</u>. We see his hand behind the growth and the blessings we have experienced. Listen to how God describes David's story to David: *"I took you from the pasture, from following the sheep, that you should be prince over my people Israel. And I have been with you wherever you went and have cut off all your enemies from before you. And I will make for you a great name, like the name of the great ones of the earth"*(2 Sam 7:8-9). God takes David back to his roots—to young days of keeping sheep, through the battles with Goliath and the Philistines, through his years of running from Saul.

And David responds in prayer: *"Who am I, O Lord GOD, and what is my house, that you have brought me thus far? And yet this was a small thing in your eyes, O Lord GOD"* (2 Sam 7:18-19). David is left praising God, humbled afresh.

Practice humility. Remember your roots. Spend some time in thought about your past. If possible, talk to someone who remembers you as a child. Visit your hometown. Thank your parents if you have the opportunity.

Remember your roots. Think about the ways you have struggled in different life stages. Consider the people who were patient with you. Dwell on the depth of your rebellion against God. Tap into the emotion and shame of what you have done. Spend time praising God for saving you from your sin and from yourself. Meditate on where you are now and how God has brought you there.

Practice humility. Remember your roots.

Field Notes

- <u>Watch out for rose-colored glasses</u>. Engaging with the past can be challenging. We tend to either edit out the bad or the good to make a more homogenous story. After I wrote this chapter, I returned to my hometown. I was surprised to talk to people I had known as a child and find their impressions—about our town, our church, and even me—were far different from my own. Remembering our roots is only valuable when we are seeing things clearly.

- <u>The past is not for living</u>. It is good to go back to the past for a visit, but we have to return to the present. Remembering our spiritual past may make us yearn for our old sins and way of life. Remembering our physical past may make us wistful for an easier time. Yet neither of these sensations is particularly helpful. Remember: be humbled, and then get back to living in the present.

CHAPTER 25: NOTICE YOUR GREEN GRASS

W E CAN BE RESTLESS AND DISCONTENT, even in the best situations. We tend to think that true happiness is just around the next bend—when some circumstance will finally fall into place and things will be perfect. When the kids get out of diapers—or can clean up after themselves—or can drive—or get out of the house—*then* we'll be happy. Just a little more money or a little nicer home or a little more credit from the boss is all that stands between us and contentment.

Our world encourages this. In a consumer economy, every advertising message tells us that our lives are miserable and incomplete because we lack their product or service. Social media broadcasts how great the lives of all of our friends are—their perfect children, awesome vacations, and fun parties (minus all their hard times, of course). We feel like we are missing something and are always just a step away from the life we really want.

This restlessness can seep over into our spiritual lives as well, where we become discontent with where we are and what God has done for us.

Humility teaches us to notice our own green grass.

The Biblical Connection

Paul shows us that contentment can power us through the worst situations. Writing from prison, Paul tells the Philippians, *"I have learned in whatever situation I am to be content. I know how to be brought low, and I know how to abound. In any and every circumstance, I have learned the secret of facing plenty and hunger, abundance and need. I can do all things through Christ who strengthens me"*(Phil 4:11-13). The spirit of contentment can thrive in any circumstance. We can always choose it. In all situations, there are some things that are not ideal and some things to rejoice in and appreciate. If we are waiting for perfect circumstances to make us content, we will never get there.

This is the reason that in the same breath, Paul urges the Philippians to make some choices about their mental focus. *"Do not be anxious about anything, but in everything by prayer and supplication with thanksgiving let your requests be made known to God. And the peace of God, which surpasses all understanding, will guard your hearts and your minds in Christ Jesus"*(Phil 4:6-7). Any situation can produce anxiety if we allow it, but we can also choose not to be anxious. In its place Paul advocates *thanksgiving*—noticing our own green grass. Instead of asking, "What has God *not* done?", we wonder, "What *has* God done?".

Paul instructs us to make different choices about our thought patterns. *"Finally, brothers, whatever is true, whatever is honorable, whatever is just, whatever is pure, whatever is lovely, whatever is commendable, if there is any excellence, if there is anything worthy of praise, think about these things"*(Phil 4:8). Every situation will hold things that are positive and negative. By telling us what to think about, Paul is also telling us what *not* to think about. Focus on all the good around you—all the things that have been done for you—all the people who love you—all that you have to look forward to—rather than what is not ideal. Notice your green grass.

This is a strong contrast to focusing on what we do *not* have—which Scripture warns against. Contentment is often juxtaposed with the love of money—which presumes that we want more money. Paul tells Timothy, "*But if we have food and clothing, with these we will be content. But those who desire to be rich fall into temptation, into a snare...*"(1 Tim 6:8-9). We can be content with a standard of living far below what we usually expect. But if we focus on getting more and more, contentment will remain elusive. "*Keep your life free from love of money, and be content with what you have, for he has said, 'I will never leave you nor forsake you'*"(Heb 13:5). The writer pushes us away from fixating on what we lack and toward noticing "*what you have*": the physical things we need for life and a promise that God will always be with us so that we don't have to fear.

God targets this restlessness when he prohibits covetousness in the Ten Commandments: "*And you shall not covet your neighbor's wife. And you shall not desire your neighbor's house, his field, or his male servant, or his female servant, his ox, or his donkey, or anything that is your neighbor's*"(Deut 5:21). When we start focusing on what others have—and wanting it rather than rejoicing with them for their blessings—we lose our focus. We become unhappy. Our spirit grows sour. We fail to notice our green grass.

Why Is This Hard?

We tend to receive blessings from God, enjoy them, and then get used to them. <u>It is hard to keep gratitude fresh</u>. We are able to adapt very quickly to new situations—a skill that can be good and bad. This failure to notice what has already been done for us sometimes leads us to believe we deserve far more than what we have, making us restless.

Occasionally we ask for and receive blessings from God, but in a different way than we expected. I have often found that I even forget that I prayed about something that I later received and came to take for granted. <u>Poor memories and a lack of discernment about God's working</u> contribute to our restlessness.

<u>We get bored and seek novelty</u>. We long to be stimulated and experience new things. This impulse can have a lot of benefits— driving us to achieve, helping us to deepen our relationships, and making life fresh. Yet when ordinary life starts to become a little too ordinary, we begin to think that some kind of change would make everything better. We start to look around.

We also fail to notice what is good about our situation because we <u>are too busy focusing on others and *their* situations</u>. We compare ourselves to them and become jealous. We are not sure they deserve what they have (but are pretty sure that we do). It is hard to notice our own green grass when there are so many interesting things on the other side of the fence.

Most of all, focusing on our blessings is hard because <u>we tend to think that it is our *circumstances* that are the problem</u>. People are not saying and doing what we want. We don't quite have enough money to get all the things we want. Some things are inconvenient and frustrating. We convince ourselves that all the problems are outside of us. We may even come to believe that adjusting our mindset about those things is merely glossing over the real issue. Something just needs to change. We continue to grow frustrated about what is not ideal and overlook the blessings right in front of us.

How Does This Help with Humility?

At heart, this <u>discontentment is a pride problem</u>. It is our ego whispering to us that we *deserve* everything we could possibly dream of to make us happy. Somehow, we deserve to have all the obstacles removed, to never be inconvenienced, to never have an unpleasant interaction, to have everyone like us, to never lack anything. Who has ever lived this life? To break the spell of this aspect of pride, we need to notice our own green grass.

God has richly blessed each of us. What *has* he done for us? How is the grass green right where we are? What factors about our situation—family, finances, faith, education, occupation, maturity, wisdom—are good? Counting our blessings will <u>calm the restless spirit</u>. It reminds us that it's OK if we don't achieve everything in the world, don't know everything, and don't have the most money. We have still been tremendously blessed and have all that we need. *"Be content with what you have."*

Counting our blessings will <u>naturally lead us into gratitude and praise</u>. If we feel little connection to God or energy for worship, it is likely that this is the trouble spot. We have forgotten all that he has done for us. Noticing our green grass changes us from spoiled children into thankful beneficiaries. We see God's hand in every aspect of our lives. We want to thank and praise him. We remember our place.

Noticing our green grass also helps quell comparisons. God has blessed us specially and uniquely. Others do not have all the blessings we have, nor do we have what they have. That's OK! We can be thankful and at peace, knowing the rich blessings we have received.

Focusing on God's blessings to us reminds us that our happiness is not what's important about life. God will meet our needs, but there is no promise of continual comfort and ease. That's not what life is about. God has higher plans for us. Very often growth and progress require pain and challenge. There is maturity and wisdom in accepting the blessing of the place, time, and situation in which we live. We lower ourselves and accept both the good and the bad from God.

Practice humility. What has God done in your life? Notice your green grass.

Field Notes

- <u>Count your blessings thoroughly</u>. List out the blessings that you have been given. Start with your own life. Thank God that the needs of your body are met. Seek out the good in your physical situation. Branch out to your family. What is good about your station in life? What people are there in your life that sharpen you? How is God using you to challenge and bless others? Where do you see God at work? Move out to your church family. What good do you see there? Keep listing. What growth do you see in yourself and others? What long-term goals are you inching toward? What do you have that is beyond what you need? What makes you happy? Name your blessings one by one.

- <u>The real challenge here is maintaining positive focus</u>. When I am especially thoughtful and intentional, I find that I am very content and thankful for my life. But when my attention to my own green grass drifts, I become negative and unhappy again. The good news is that over time, I find that I have developed a more natural instinct of seeing the good in a situation, person, or interaction. Keep noticing what's good!

CHAPTER 26: SHINE THE SPOTLIGHT ON OTHERS

A T TIMES OUR ACTIONS GAIN ATTENTION. While this is encouraging when we are doing right, we can easily become consumed with being in the spotlight and succeeding in the court of public opinion. We are never satisfied with the level of notoriety and respect we receive. We are never able to let others have the glory.

Humility means shining the spotlight on others.

The Biblical Connection

Prior to Jesus' coming, John the Baptist gains a great following by preaching the need for repentance because the kingdom is at hand. John is a tremendous example of humility because he never lets his popularity mislead him about his role in God's work. He continually points to Jesus, denigrating himself: *"After me comes he who is mightier than I, the strap of whose sandals I am not worthy to stoop down and untie"*(Mark 1:7). When a delegation comes from the

Jews in Jerusalem to nail down his identity, he denies that he is the Christ, Elijah, or the Prophet (John 1:19-21). He describes himself only as *"the voice of one crying out in the wilderness, 'Make straight the way of the Lord'"*(John 1:23).

Yet there is no greater challenge than when Jesus begins to make more disciples than John (John 4:1). John's disciples are concerned (and a little threatened) by this. They lament that *"all are going to him"*(John 3:26). John corrects their perspective: *"The one who has the bride is the bridegroom. The friend of the bridegroom, who stands and hears him, rejoices greatly at the bridegroom's voice. Therefore this joy of mine is now complete. He must increase, but I must decrease'"*(John 3:29-30). Even now, John refuses to make this into a contest between him and Jesus. He knows his place.

We must make special note of John's phrase: *"He must increase, but I must decrease."* John shines the spotlight on Jesus at his own expense. Jesus' mission is greater than John's. John is not threatened by this. He knows that he and Jesus are on the same team. And when Jesus increases, John's joy increases. This is humility.

Moses also shows this willingness to celebrate others. While leading the people in the desert, Moses is upset by their continual complaining. God responds by giving him seventy elders to help him bear the load of leadership. He puts his Spirit on them and they begin to prophesy in the camp. *"And Joshua the son of Nun, the assistant of Moses from his youth, said, 'My lord Moses, stop them.' But Moses said to him, 'Are you jealous for my sake? Would that all the LORD's people were prophets, that the LORD would put his Spirit on them!'"*(Num 11:28-29). Joshua is concerned that these men prophesying would in some way diminish Moses in his role as

God's spokesman and leader. Moses seems to laugh at this idea. *"Are you jealous for my sake?"* How could Joshua be more upset for Moses than Moses is? Instead, Moses wishes that all the people were prophets. Not only would God's glory increase, but Moses would have less of a burden to bear. Moses' humility springs from the fact that *any honor given to anyone else only helps the cause.* Why should we feel threatened when others are honored for doing good?

Paul excels at this too. Even though he is a lightning rod for a lot of the conflict surrounding the gospel in the first century, he is often willing to shine the spotlight on others. He commends Timothy to the Philippians: *"For I have no one like him, who will be genuinely concerned for your welfare. For they all seek their own interests, not those of Jesus Christ. But you know Timothy's proven worth, how as a son with a father he has served with me in the gospel"* (Phil 2:20-22). Paul does more than simply speak kindly of Timothy; he is giving a full-throated endorsement of all his work. He wants them to see Timothy for what he is and value him. Paul is not at all threatened by Timothy's work; he is furthered by it.

There is blessing in highlighting others while allowing ourselves to play second fiddle.

Why Is This Hard?

<u>We like the spotlight!</u> We like and want credit, especially when we feel that we are responsible for something. One of the most galling experiences in our culture is when someone swoops in and takes credit for our work. Deliberately calling attention to others means diminishing our own accomplishments and choosing to sign up for unfairness.

Putting a spotlight on others is hard because we easily get jealous. This is the undercurrent in the biblical stories. John's disciples and Joshua are jealous of the attention these upstarts are receiving. We often presume that the attention others receive is attention we will never receive. They will get glory and we won't. We will lose face. There is a high level of pride here.

Sometimes we reach the point where we begin to tear others down because we feel that they don't deserve the spotlight. We can grow so consumed by this feeling that we do not see it in ourselves. We just let the perceived inequity fester into bitterness and anger.

Sharing the spotlight is hard because in Christian circles, we also feel that using *our* talents is how we fulfill God's will for us. He gave each of us specific gifts to use in his service. Yet if someone else leads and uses his gifts, our own contribution will be diminished. We may even leave a church because we are not being "used" enough. Our pride can masquerade as the noble impulse of using God's gifts.

This is also hard because we may have to learn a new skill: how to say positive things about others without agenda—without a "but"(see chapter 9). This can be quite challenging if we are not accustomed to giving unqualified praise.

How Does This Help with Humility?

John's statement "*he must increase, but I must decrease*" speaks to a natural lowering. When we shine the spotlight on others, we fade (at least for the moment) into the background. Our job is only to lift others up. There is humility in accepting a *supporting* role rather than insisting that we must be the star of the show.

Shining the spotlight on others <u>puts the focus on the goal instead of on me</u>. Each of the biblical examples stresses this. John is concerned about God's kingdom, not himself. Moses is focused on God spreading his word and Spirit. Paul wants Timothy to continue his good work. This spirit reminds us that we are on the same team with those who are doing right. If we tear them down, we only hurt the team.

Shining the spotlight on others—sincerely and without agenda—<u>defuses jealousy</u>. We learn to look for the good in others and what they are doing, rather than making a case for why they don't deserve attention.

Shining the spotlight on others also reminds us that <u>there is a bigger cause than our own pleasure and validation</u>. The time will come when we will fade into the background—whether by our deaths, the ravages of age, or merely our relative unimportance. Why not learn to accept this now? If we share the load (and the credit it brings) now, we prepare the next generation to find their footing and grow into a new role. This process is essential for our jobs, churches, and homes. The good of the group necessitates forward thinking and minimizing ourselves.

Practice humility. Find others who are doing good. Endorse them. Enlist their help in efforts that will help their talents to stand out. Speak well of them. Give them time in the spotlight. Encourage others to go to them. See the good that they are doing and bring it into the open.

Practice humility. Shine the spotlight on others.

Field Notes

- <u>Not everyone is gracious in the spotlight</u>. One of the most galling experiences is when we yield to others, giving them praise and attention, and they assume that they deserve it. *They already thought they were better than we are—and they are just happy that we finally acknowledged it!* This is also a humbling experience, but one that we might not expect. We give way to others when they are deserving of appreciation, yet we cannot guarantee they will behave well.

- <u>Not everyone wants to be in the spotlight</u>. Sometimes others resist our efforts to appreciate and praise them. It may be that they are trying to deflect our compliments (see chapter 21) so that they don't contribute to their own pride. Or it may be that they are just shy and don't enjoy being noticed. Whatever the case, we should be aware of their wishes and work to encourage them quietly in the meantime.

CHAPTER 27: WAIT

ADVANCES IN TECHNOLOGY have made it so that we can do more faster than ever before. Trips that a century ago would have taken a week now take hours. We can communicate instantly with almost anyone in the world at any time. We can know any fact without opening a book. We have instant oatmeal.

But something is lost in all this rush. We lose a sense of the *value* of that communication, learning, and travel. Instead of living amazed with the incredible world we inhabit, we grow bored with it. And whenever our expectation of instant gratification is thwarted—like when we come up against processes we cannot rush—we grow angry and petulant. We lose the ability to wait well.

Practice humility. Wait.

The Biblical Connection

In the Old Testament, God's people are frequently urged to *"wait on the LORD."* Sometimes they wait while patiently anticipating God's justice: *"Be still before the LORD and wait patiently for him; fret not yourself over the one who prospers in his way, over the man who carries out evil devices!...For the evildoers shall be cut off, but those who wait for the LORD shall inherit the land"* (Psalm 37:7, 9). Evil people appear to prosper, but we endure this temporary unfairness because God will someday restore order.

Sometimes there is imminent danger facing God's people and they await his deliverance. David begins Psalm 27 assailed by people who want to harm him (Psalm 27:2), yet he closes the psalm by chiding himself: *"I believe that I shall look upon the goodness of the LORD in the land of the living! Wait for the LORD; be strong, and let your heart take courage; wait for the LORD!"* (Psalm 27:13-14).

But most importantly, Old Testament characters wait on God to fulfill his promises to them. Abraham waits and wanders for decades before seeing the promised child. David waits for many years before he is made king as he had been promised. Israel comes into the Promised Land centuries after it is promised to them. And it is this sense of waiting that sustains the people of Israel through centuries of exile and messianic waiting. *"Even youths shall faint and be weary, and young men shall fall exhausted; but they who wait for the LORD shall renew their strength; they shall mount up with wings like eagles; they shall run and not be weary; they shall walk and not faint"* (Isa 40:30-31).

There is an elementary observation in order here: If Bible people were expected to wait—sometimes for years—for justice, salvation, and God to fulfill direct promises—how much more can I wait on my burrito or my internet connection? The difference is jarring.

In the New Testament, we do not wait for the coming of the Messiah, but his second coming. *"Be patient, therefore, brothers, until the coming of the Lord. See how the farmer waits for the precious fruit of the earth, being patient about it, until it receives the early and the late rains. You also, be patient. Establish your hearts, for the coming of the Lord is at hand"* (James 5:7-8). James advocates patience because we don't know the exact moment when Jesus will return. There are things we will live with because we know that someday they will be changed. This is the heart of good waiting.

Of course, the Bible also emphasizes patience with people. Sometimes we have to wait on people to grow. So we need to live *"with all humility and gentleness, with patience, bearing with one another in love"* (Eph 4:2) as we teach our fellow disciples *"until we all attain to the unity of the faith and of the knowledge of the Son of God, to mature manhood"* (Eph 4:13). We grow together—and that requires both patience and humility. No one is perfect yet and we must learn to await further stages of growth.

Behind all the Bible's instruction on waiting is the reality that there are processes beyond our control. Like the farmer, some things can't be rushed. Like a parent watching a child grow, some things take time. We don't control when or how God acts. We are at the mercy of forces outside our power—and we must embrace the humility of waiting.

Why Is This Hard?

Waiting is hard because <u>it is unpleasant</u>. We have things that we want or need, but we must delay gratification and satisfaction. Living for a period of time in which we feel incomplete is a frustrating experience.

Waiting is hard because <u>it is often indefinite</u>. We can handle unpleasantness when we have assurances that it will only last a little while, but waiting for an indeterminate amount of time can be agonizing. We can adjust to traffic when we're certain it's a 20-minute backup; if we only see miles of taillights, we despair.

We usually do better when we understand *why* we have to wait, yet these <u>explanations aren't always given</u>. This must be why we are willing to patiently in a long line (where we see the other people) but cannot abide a few seconds of delay in our internet connection (because we don't understand what's happening). Many situations in life—and in spiritual things—demand waiting without any clear reasons.

Waiting is also particularly hard <u>when we see some people who don't have to wait</u>. We might make peace with the idea of waiting to own a home—working hard and carefully saving to make a down payment. But that peace is dashed when we see someone born into money who doesn't have to wait or work for anything. We are creatures of comparison and when we have to wait while others don't, waiting becomes that much harder.

How Does This Help with Humility?

Waiting <u>helps us to acknowledge our limitations</u>. There are some situations in which we are not in control. We cannot push a button and speed them up. We cannot rush raising children. We cannot hurry along our communion with God. We cannot mature faster. It takes time to save money and invest in relationships. We are not powerless, but we are severely limited. It's OK to wait.

Waiting means that <u>our concerns and needs are not that urgent</u>. We can live with discomfort. It is often through this discomfort that we strengthen our ability to endure difficulty (James 1:2-4).

We also appreciate things far more when we've had to wait to get them.

We face choices daily that demand the ability to wait. Will I save this money or spend it? Will I buy this thing that I can't afford yet or will I wait? Will I eat this delicious food or try to lose weight? In these small decisions, we exercise our waiting muscles. Then, when longer-term problems arise, we are prepared. We are ready to embrace waiting for a solution to our physical pain—or waiting for God to soften someone's heart—or waiting for the slow process of financial recovery. Life teaches us that all choices have eventual consequences—*"whatever one sows, that will he also reap"* (Gal 6:7). But waiting prepares us for what we are truly waiting for: *"The one who sows to the Spirit will from the Spirit reap eternal life. And let us not grow weary of doing good, for in due season we will reap, if we do not give up"* (Gal 6:8-9). Humility is in trusting this promise, diligently sowing, and waiting on the Lord.

Practice humility. Take opportunities to wait as chances to learn humility. Reject impulses. Calm your spirit. Accept the discomfort of things not being ideal.

Practice humility. Wait.

Field Notes

- <u>Waiting is deeply countercultural</u>. Whether it is waiting in a line for some service or waiting at a stoplight, Americans are not a patient people. Our obsession with convenience makes us restless and easily bored. As I focused on waiting, I found myself constantly picking up my phone to entertain me (even at red lights!) in any moment of waiting. I noticed my children complaining at every moment of boredom. Our society is deeply concerned with things being *fast*—from ER times to food prep. Gaining humility by waiting will make us feel like a throw-back to a much simpler time.

CONCLUSION: IS IT I, LORD?

AS JESUS EATS THE LAST SUPPER with his disciples, he issues a shocking prophecy: *"Truly, I say to you, one of you will betray me"*(Matt 26:21). This surely brings the room down. The meal takes on an ominous tone. *"And they were very sorrowful and began to say to him one after another, 'Is it I, Lord?'"*(Matt 26:22). All twelve of them must now examine themselves: *Could he be talking about me?*

When Scripture describes and condemns pride, the goal is not simply for us to feel better about God judging people we don't like. The goal is that we sit alongside the disciples and ask, "Is it I, Lord?" *Could he be talking about me?*

Pride is insidious and devious. We humble ourselves before God, but then we become proud of our humility and we're back to step 1. We address our pride for the moment, but then we find it taking a new form and we rediscover our need for humility. We look back on past times where we felt humble and do not recognize that we may be in a different place now.

I have had the opportunity to preach and speak directly to people who were consumed by pride. Everyone recognized it and correctly diagnosed it—*except them.* I then had the surreal experience of being critiqued about my pride sermon by a proud person. The horrible irony is that in the process I have fallen prey to my own pride. Even as I preach on pride to prideful people who respond pridefully, I recoil at their attitude and display my own pride. The cycle goes on.

Somehow we manage to continually underestimate pride's power and subtlety. Cutting through this morass is the simple, bruising question: *Is it I, Lord? Could he be talking about me?*

What Is the Point?

Proud people are insufferable; they are also vulnerable. Jealousy, anger, and dishonesty can make inroads in a proud heart. Worse, no one can talk to us about these sins because we are too proud to listen. Humility is not some abstract goal for self-improvement. We need it *desperately.*

To loosen pride's grip on us, we must acknowledge the areas where it reigns. Throughout this book, we have seen pride's forms: self-focus, condescension, complacency, complaining, and impatience. Its manifestations will be unique to us. My hope is that these thoughts will heighten your awareness of pride in your own thinking, speech, and treatment of others. You may notice pride more easily in others—but beware condescending to them! The power of these practices will rest in our willingness to see pride in ourselves and root it out.

Certain practices can help us push back pride and advance toward humility. They cannot be checked off as complete when we have done them once. They are ongoing pursuits. Some will be easier than others. Some may be no trouble at all. Others will be deeply challenging. Do not be deterred by the difficulty. It is likely a proof that there is a problem.

Humility only works when we practice it. Praising humility, studying it, and decrying the lack of it are not the same as *doing*. These practices help us by bringing focused attention to the problem and disciplining our thinking and behavior to ensure that we are in line with God's expectations for us. Calling our pride what it is and fighting it regularly can give us small victories. We get a little stronger—a little more used to serving—a little less self-absorbed—a little less entitled.

What will you do—*today*—to grow more humble?

Works Cited

Brooks, David. *The Road to Character*. Random House, 2015.

Kovacs, Judith L., ed. *1 Corinthians: Interpreted by Early Christian Medieval Commentators*. Eerdmans, 2005.

Lewis, C.S. *Mere Christianity. The Complete C.S. Lewis Signature Classics*. HarperOne, 2002.

Lewis, C.S. *Reflections on the Psalms*. HarperOne, 2017.

Lewis, C.S. *The Screwtape Letters. The Complete C.S. Lewis Signature Classics*. HarperOne, 2002.

Wilken, Robert Louis. *The Spirit of Early Christian Thought*. Yale University Press, 2003.

Worthington, Jr., Everett. *Humility: The Quiet Virtue*. Templeton Foundation Press, 2007.

Yancey, Philip. *The Bible Jesus Read*. Zondervan, 1999.

A Note from the Author

Thanks for reading *Humility Practice*! I would greatly appreciate your feedback on the book. Would you take a moment to review the book on Amazon? Amazon reviews ensure that more people find *Humility Practice* and also help me know what readers find helpful or problematic about the book. You can review by searching for the book on Amazon's site and scrolling down to the "Write a review" button.

For more information about other titles, visit my website at jacobhudgins.com.

Thanks!

Jacob Hudgins

Made in United States
Orlando, FL
04 May 2022

17536540R00119

The true nature of a Bible

After opening a Bible, locate the "Table of Contents" and scan it carefully. You will, of course, encounter a list of items. Somewhere within this list, if you have a Christian bible, you will find one list of writings bearing the title "Old Testament" and another list of writings titled "New Testament." The writings that appear in these two lists are the inspired writings that are contained in the Bible! If you take the time to compare one bible with another, you will discover that there is no total agreement between all of the churches as to which books are and which are not inspired. You will also discover that a Jewish bible does not possess a New Testament and that the inspired writings that it does contain have been put in a different order than they are in the Christian Bible. We will treat this matter in more detail later.

With the exception of the sacred "books," everything else in a Bible is ordinary material which is entirely the work of human beings and that has no direct, divine participation.

A Bible, therefore, contains two fundamentally different types of material. On the one hand, the sacred writings have, in some way, God for their author. On the other hand, a lot of added common material that is entirely the work of human beings working without divine assistance in a direct sense.

In spite of the fact that Christians and Jews believe that the sacred writings in a Bible are inspired by God, there is no visual indication in the Table of Contents to indicate that the every book listed actually contains material of two fundamentally different types – the original words of Scripture and the added human notes, commentaries, introductions, etc. This lack of distinction can mislead people. Some people mistakenly believe ordinary writing to be inspired. Your authors have known people who believed that the commentary in the margins of the inspired writings was inspired in the same manner as the biblical text itself!

In moving onward from this point, let us first explore the mystery that is inspiration. We will take up the "study stuff" when we begin to study the actual texts in detail.